WILL I SURVIVE?
THE PURPOSE AND PROCESS IN LIFE

BRUCE J. BARTEL

PUBLISHED BY
OUR WRITTEN LIVES OF HOPE, LLC

Our Written Lives provides publishing services
for independent authors. www.owlofhope.com.

All rights reserved. No part of this publication may be reproduced,
stored in a retrieval system, or transmitted in any form or by any
means, without the permission of the copyright holders.

Copyright ©2015 Bruce J. Bartel

Cover photo created by Crystal Bailey, a composit
of photos used with permission from Shutterstock.com

Library of Congress Cataloging-in-Publication Data
Library of Congress Control Number: 2015903080
Bartel, Bruce J. 1959—

ISBN: 978-1-942923-00-8 (paperback)

Unless otherwise noted, scripture quotations are from
the New King James Version®, "NKJV™"
Copyright © 1982 by Thomas Nelson, Inc.
Used by permission. All rights reserved.

WILL I SURVIVE?
THE PURPOSE AND PROCESS IN LIFE

FOREWORD

In his book, Will I Survive?, Bruce Bartel takes us through the process of change and growth, which results in our reflecting the image of God. Sometimes we make the mistake of thinking at some point we "arrived," or we "peaked" in our walk with God. Not so.

What will you do when hardships and disappointments come? How we respond in difficult times can make us or break us. God is trying to teach us something through these challenges. Are you willing to learn and grow through the process, or will you give up?

We see in Romans 8:28, "all things work together for good." Verse 29 tells us for what purpose: that we would be formed and changed into His image. God's hand upon us results in change into a deeper Christ-like image. We can't do it without Him, and He will not do it without us. The word change in Romans 8:29 comes from a Greek word which means mold.

In this book, Bruce masterfully shows us how to allow God to mold us into His image. It's a great and spiritually challenging read.

Pastor Ron Libby

ENDORSEMENTS

Negative life experiences impact us in a variety of ways on a variety of levels. Understanding how devastating life events have affected us is only a minuscule portion of our spiritual healing and deliverance. Discerning how to navigate the emotional labyrinth of restoration takes a sensitive, guiding hand of spiritual experience.

Bruce has humbly presented personal vulnerabilities and revelatory insights, which offer a beacon of hope to lead other wounded souls out of darkness. I applaud his courage of ministry. **—Tony Bailey**, Pastor, Bible College Instructor, International Conference Speaker, Author

The difficult things of life can overshadow the good times. Sickness causes us to forget what it felt like to be well. In this book, you will read encouraging words from the pen of a man that has faced the ugly turns of life head-on. Through his experiences and trials, he learned to navigate the choppy waters of unpleasant circumstances through an ever deepening relationship with Jesus Christ. This book is birthed from those experiences. Read, learn and be victorious. **—Steve Carrington**, Pastor, District Superintendent-New Mexico/Western Texas

I met Evangelist Bruce Bartel over 25 years ago when he came to minister in our church on a couple of occasions. His ministry was genuine, sincere and led of the Spirit of God. This book is not a lecture, but it comes out of the heart of experience and is truthful about what we must go through in order to become what the Master desires us to be. The process may be difficult and painful, but the end result produces what will bring peace and will glorify God.
—**Paul Graham**, Multi-congregational Pastor, Montreal Canada; International Conference Speaker

Whether you are a seasoned traveler or just began your walk with God, the principles in this treatise are paramount to a well charted course. The author takes great care in not only providing Biblical insight, but also challenging the reader to apply them.

Bruce Bartel has managed to get the reader to examine their own vulnerability to life's challenges, while providing the insights necessary to prevent them from becoming a casualty along the way. It's a comfortable read with personal and candid reflections.
—**Ric S. Gonzalez**, Pastor, Chicago Metro Church Planter, International Conference Speaker and Evangelist

I have known Bruce Bartel for over 30 years. He is a student of the Word, devoted to living for God with a strong desire and determination to keep his life above reproach. His life is a testimony on how to handle life's curves with integrity and honor. You will find his writings interesting, thought provoking, and motivating! **—Arden Bustard,** Pastor at Large, Canada; International Evangelist

Bruce Bartel is not only a marvelous friend, but he is also an excellent preacher and is now proving himself to be an accomplished writer. His ability to weather some difficult times in life has qualified him to be greatly used of God. **—Mike Conn,** Pastor, District Superintendent-Kansas, Author

For anyone who has been through the dry places, had to climb a mountain, or go through a deep valley, this book is a must read. It will help you find your way through those times. **—David Shatwell**, Pastor, Oklahoma, Conference Speaker, International Evangelist

As in life, every hill has an up and a balancing down. Victim precedes victor, trial precedes triumph and helplessness precedes miracles. This book needed to be written and comes from both Biblical research and experience. With over 20 years of friendship, I have personally witnessed Bruce's Godly example and spiritual sensitivity. He lives what he believes and practices what he preaches. I know this book will enlighten many and be a blessing to all. **—Larry Sims**, Pastor, Vancouver Canada

DEDICATION

This book is affectionately dedicated to
my Father and Mother,
Jacob and Mary Bartel.

Mom, thanks for all the sacrifices you've made for me.

Dad, I always enjoy talking with you.
When it came to advice, you would always ask
me questions and help me think things through. I
always seemed to make good decisions
after our discussions.
Thanks for being my friend.
Thanks for being my Father.

ACKNOWLEDGEMENTS

First and foremost I am forever indebted to the grace and mercy of my Lord and my God, Jesus the Christ. His name is above all names and at the name of Jesus every knee shall bow. I gladly, willingly and wholeheartedly bow my very being to You. Without You, I want and can do nothing. I acknowledge, align and yield myself to You, the One true God of the Bible.

To Glen and Bev Nystrom – your kindness, generosity, and hospitality help save me. You were there when most were not. Thanks for inviting and sharing your home with me. The beautiful views of the Rocky Mountains from your study, help bring this book to life. I am forever in your debt. Bev, thanks for your valued input and perspective in editing this book.

To Crystal Bailey – thanks for your support and the many hours of help you put in throughout this entire project. You are specially gifted. I am eternally thankful I met you.

To Ron Libby – thanks for being there. Your words of wisdom and support ministered to my mind and spirit. You helped keep me above the water line in life. Thanks for your friendship.

To those who believed in me enough to endorse this book: Tony Bailey, Steve Carrington, Paul Graham, Ric Gonzalez, Arden Bustard, Mike Conn, David Shatwell and Larry Sims. Thanks for your friendship. You are of value to me.

To Chester Wright – thanks for the seeds sown and insights garnered over the years. This book was planted in one of those Manifest Sessions.

To Our Written Lives, and Rachael Hartman – thank you for bringing this manuscript to print. You have grown into a woman of God.

CONTENTS

Preface _____ 16

LIFE'S CHALLENGE

Chapter 1: So What Now?_____ 21
Chapter 2: The Purpose & Process _____ 33

BREAD-MAKING

Chapter 3: Sowing_____ 53
Chapter 4: Reaping _____ 69
Chapter 5: Chaff _____ 85
Chapter 6: The Fire _____ 101
Chapter 7: Storage _____ 127
Chapter 8: Flour & Dough _____ 143

SURVIVING & THRIVING

Chapter 9: Living in Two Places _____ 155
Chapter 10: Releasing the Miracle _____ 167
Chapter 11: The Two Hands of God _____ 187
Chapter 12: Whatsoever He Says _____ 213

PREFACE

When crisis overwhelmed my life, I found myself desperately searching for answers. I was consumed with emotional pain and spiritual bewilderment. As time went on, I began to stop focusing on the pain and circumstances, and started to look to Jesus simply and deliberately. I knew my crisis was not going away overnight. I needed to start putting one foot in front of the other, and consciously walk to Jesus.

Life happens to us all. It's what you do with what happens to you that will determine your outcome. Always remember, it is not who you are, but to whom you belong that is your constant security and comfort.

This is not a tale of woe and I have no axe to grind. The Bible is clear, the rain falls on the just and the unjust; good things happen to bad people and bad things happen to good people. Though life may bring questions about the acts of God, I pray it never brings questions about your relationship with Him. With a personal committed relationship with your Creator, you can walk through what other men burn in. Just ask Shadrach, Meshach and Abednego.

Life begins at the end our comfort zone. If we will not change, we will not grow. If we are not growing, we are not really living. Growth demands a temporary surrender of security. It often means the giving up of the familiar in order to step into the new you, where Jesus is leading and molding.

One of my constant reminders in life has been the revelation that what happens to me is less significant than what happens within me. You and I are not judged in eternity by a single act, but by a life time. Don't abort the purpose and process Jesus has for you. Keep walking and talking with Him.

It is my sincere prayer this book will bring revelation, understanding, comfort and freedom into your life and walk with God. There is no courage without fear. Danger and uncertainty are all around us; however, fear is optional. Be strong in the Lord Jesus; He is praying for you (Luke 22:32; John 17:20).

May Grace and Peace be multiplied to you.

B.J. Bartel

LIFE'S CHALLENGE

1
SO WHAT NOW?

Will I survive? It is a question going across many minds today. If you've lived any time at all, the question is there, consciously or subconsciously. Why is so much bad happening to me? Where is God in all of the chaos?

Have you ever gone through a time in your life when all seemed off balance and out of focus? Everything that could go wrong did! Frustration turned into alienation, which finally dipped into depression. What did you do when crisis hit, making you feel imprisoned? Did you use the moment to seek God, or to mull over your misfortune and brood in silent anger? Your answer will determine your salvation or your demise.

Our human nature always wants to figure things out, to find meaning and purpose in everything. Somehow, if you knew the purpose of "things" in the past, they would be somewhat more bearable. You could handle it better, if only you could see your way clearly.

To the non-believer, a crisis is an opportunity for God to work. Non-believers tend to be more open to the idea and concept of God when they are in crisis. To the

WILL I SURVIVE?

believer, on the other hand, a crisis is an opportunity for satan to work. Somehow, believers have the idea nothing bad will ever happen to them because of their faith. So when life happens, and it does, questions, fears and doubts arise challenging their faith in God and providing a devil's paradise.

This book is not is not meant to be philosophical, theoretical or theological. It is a practical book that will meet you where you live, in everyday life and everyday situations. I find great revelation in a statement made in one of the Minor Prophets: ***My people are destroyed for lack of knowledge*** (Hosea 4:6).

> **My people are destroyed for lack of knowledge.**
> **Hosea 4:6**

With knowledge comes understanding. With understanding comes comfort, strength and courage to keep going. Without knowledge or purpose you are lost. It's only a matter of time before you are eventually destroyed and consumed in your perceived reality. You are no longer a person led by destiny. You just exist and are susceptible to your fallen nature.

You must realize your trials and tribulations in life are an opportunity to renew your mind in the knowledge of God, not in the circumstances. Your eternity demands you diligently keep your thoughts and mind on Jesus, the Author and Finisher of your faith. Thoughts become words and words become reality.

Often, a crisis is only an opportunity for you to grow in your relationship and reliance on your Lord and

SO WHAT NOW?

Savior, Jesus Christ. Crisis reveals the inner self. It gives an opportunity for you to become the person you were meant to be. Unfortunately for many, a crisis ends up being a stumbling block taking them further from their destiny. So the question remains: are you going to become better or bitter? Will crisis make you, or break you? Is your situation a stepping-stone, or stumbling block?

> Sow a thought, and you will reap an act.
> Sow an act, and you will reap a habit.
> Sow a habit, and you will reap a character.
> Sow a character, and you will reap a destiny.

The Answer

In a very dark and lonely place of life, I found myself desperately praying and searching for answers. I was abandoned by family and friends, judged unmercifully and unjustly. My circumstances just didn't make any sense. I was consumed and rattled with emotional pain.

I tried to look to Jesus, but my pain was formidable. After the shock and tears were spent, I exhaustingly focused my attention on Jesus. Love and devotion began to pour out of my spirit for the One whom my soul loves. And I remember praying this prayer: **"Jesus, I want You more then I want the answer. You hold my world in Your hand, and I gladly and willingly yield to Your Word, Your Will, and to Your Spirit."**

WILL I SURVIVE?

After praying, the Lord spoke to my heart:

"If you will, stop looking at what you can see and let Me speak to your inner man. Let Me give you an inner vision and a dream. Then it will not matter what anyone else will say as far as what is, or is not possible."

It was during those days I began to stop focusing on the pain and circumstances, and started to look at Jesus simply and deliberately. I knew my crisis was not going away overnight. I needed to start putting one foot in front of the other, and consciously walk to Jesus. He was the only One that could help. He was the answer.

Discouragement and Depression

With revelation comes knowledge and understanding. With understanding comes the ability to handle life's situations and curves. Knowing there is a bigger picture gives a person hope and comfort. Not knowing what's happening brings discouragement and depression.

In these last days, the Lord is separating people who stand in the way of what He is going to do. His longsuffering and patience are coming to an end. He has given time and space for people to deal with their hidden sins. Now, He is revealing the concealed.

God is allowing people to see where they are vulnerable, where they are weak. He is about to transition His church into the greatest thing He has ever done, short of Calvary, but He cannot do it until the church is ready.

SO WHAT NOW?

You can deal with the struggle, if you know that you are going to come out of the situation better than when you started. It helps to know there is a purpose in the life process you find yourself in.

Discouragement and depression result in the inability to picture a positive future.

Clarity and Comfort

The purpose of this book is to help you find clarity in life. With clarity, comes peace and comfort, together with the courage and strength to continue becoming who you were meant to be. Not just a better person, but a transformed child of God, plugged into and vibrantly operating in the Body of Christ.

The will of God has not changed. There is no question that God has a good plan for your life! It's your will that is in question. Are you willing to start praying, "Lord, I will wait out this struggle as long as it takes, but I want to leave this place different than I was when I came in"...? Do you want what He wants bad enough to stop asking Him to remove life's struggle?

Jacob

Jacob wrestled with God in Genesis 32. The encounter greatly impacted him. He could have stopped wrestling and walked the rest of his life with a limp. If that was all Jacob wanted, God could have let him go. Jacob did not have to stay in the struggle, and his identity would have remained "deceiver." Who and what he was, did not change until after the fight. He stayed through the struggle, and that is when he became Israel.

Some of us have been in a struggle a long, long time. It seems it's an unending struggle. We continue praying, "Lord, I can't take much more. God, stop the struggle; stop the strain; stop the pressure." The truly amazing thing is that He will allow you to stop it. You can abort the process and stop the purpose of God from transforming you into His image. If you don't want any more then what you have now, He will stop the struggle. Then again, you will never become the person you were meant to be.

If you want to be who God knows you are, if you want to be the person He has destined you to become, then allow Him to give you the grace and strength to finish the process. Jesus will restore you. **He** will renew your strength. And you will literally be transformed into a different person than you were in the past.

Some reading this book are mentally and physically tired, so much that you have wondered if you have chronic fatigue. You can hardly wake up in the morning. You go throughout the day and all you want to do is lie down. The stress is so strong and it has taken a toll on you. You are becoming a person you've never been. What a tragedy it would be if you released yourself from the struggle and aborted the process God purposed.

SO WHAT NOW?

The Lord is saying to His Body, *"If you've got all you want and you want to break away from Me, I'm not going to try to talk you out of it anymore. I'm through begging. I'm through pleading. I'm through bargaining with you. I'm not doing that anymore. You either trust Me to shape you into My image, or you don't."*

How many of us have cried, "I can't take any more. I want out!" We must come to the place where we pray, "Lord, I want You more than I want the answer." I've personally gone through some really deep, dark places. I understand very well what it is like to cry so much that my tears stop forming, and all I can do is sigh and moan.

Some people reading this book have wanted to go to sleep at night and not wake up. I understand. But if you will stay in the process a little longer, if you will stay in the struggle a little longer, and don't abort what God is doing, things will unfold. Stop praying, "Lord, get me out of this; end it; release me from it. I can't take anymore."

Understand God has a purpose for you to actualize, and what you are about to become, you've never been before.

Every one of us must have a "nevertheless" moment multiple times. You have been in the struggle and feel as if you're at your limit with as much as you can handle. Are you are willing to stay in the struggle until you've had your nevertheless moments? Once you come to nevertheless, does

God does not try you to prove you to Himself. The trying proves you to yourself.

WILL I SURVIVE?

it mean you will never have another struggle? No. But it is in the nevertheless moments where you stop telling God what you want, and you start asking Him what **He sees**, and what **He wants**. That is where He is trying to bring you.

God, in all of His infinite wisdom and ability is shaking the church. Good Bible believers and churches across the world are feeling the same pressure. There must be a reason for it. There is a reason for it. God's math seems to always start with subtraction, but the very next step is always multiplication.

What is He cutting out of you in order to put something new into you? What is He is trying to multiply into the church? We are going to see a level of the gifts of the Spirit like we have never heard or seen before. Will you stay in the process a little longer? Will you pray, *"Not my will, but Thine, be done? Make me what I'm supposed to be, Lord, so You can do what You want, through me."*

What Do You Want?

God has not forgotten one prophetic word spoken or promise given to you. He is simply testing your will. What do you want? Do you want to come along after the miracle and collect the loaves and fishes, or do you want to be so close to Jesus that when He works, you have your hands on the miracle as soon as it happens? God will let you have either one. It is your choice.

The struggle, the battle you're going through is not for

SO WHAT NOW?

naught. It is my prayer this book will give you a second wind, a deep renewing breath and a renewal in the Spirit. I want you to find a depth in the Spirit that perhaps you have never known.

When it comes to life's struggles, could Jesus have headed them off and stopped things? Yes. Why doesn't He? Because He is trying to mold you into someone greater than you have ever been. With every advancement and promotion, there is a test. He is checking our motives and exposing what needs to change and what needs to go.

Walking With a Limp

If you just want to be a good person, you can be. But somehow, I believe there are men, women, boys and girls, like Jacob, willing to say, "I'm already going to walk with a limp. I want the anointing that goes with it. I've already been up and struggling a long night's battle. I want the dominion that goes with it. I've already been going through the pain and the pressure. I'm not leaving with an empty pocket. I'm not going to limp around and still be the person I use to be."

Jesus is trying to make you into someone greater than you have ever been.

Life is going to give you a limp, so you might as well hang on, and let the Lord change your identity! I'm tired of crying over what I don't have. I'm ready to rejoice over what I am about to have! I'm tired of weeping and sorrow as my constant companions. I'm ready to be thankful for everything that is coming!

You have been in the struggle too long to give up now. If you have been stuck in life, you are about to receive revelation and understanding as you journey with me through these chapters. You **will** find yourself somewhere in the process. Are you ready to say to Jesus, "Not my will, but Thine be done?" Do you hunger and thirst after Jesus more than you want the answers to life's questions?

I have believed in God's spiritual power, dominion and authority too long to walk away from it now. I've taken too much territory to give up now. I'm interested in seeing every prophetic word spoken over me start to unveil and come to pass. If I'm going to go through this struggle, then I want to see the rewards!

Don't Abort the Process

You know what God promised you. Don't settle for less than His promises. Stay in the fight until your identity has been completely changed. According to your faith be it unto you. I'm not about to abort the process of what He is doing. For as long as it takes, I'm in this, all the way to the end. Thus qualifying myself, to see Jesus do what He said He would do!

As we start this journey together, begin taking the old identity off. Have you ever asked the Lord, "Why

SO WHAT NOW?

not me?" and been frustrated out of your mind? Do you think the Lord can't use you after all you've been through? Perhaps some things need to change. Oh, and by the way, God does not need to change, and He's not going to change. It's you and I that need to change into His imagine, His will, by His Spirit.

> ... Let God be true and every man a liar ...
> **Romans 3:4**

God did not bury you; He planted you. You are not supposed to shrivel up and die. You were planted to grow. Will you let Him take you to a new place?

A grain of wheat has the potential of life and growth. Potential is only realized when it is planted. And a planting, if you are not sure of the purpose, feels like a burial.

God's purpose and process in our lives is for us to "become new." To 'become' is a process. It doesn't happen in a moment of time or overnight. It's a process of allowing God to take out the old and put in the new. The born again experience of John 3:5 is just the beginning. Like a newborn infant, the intention is for you and I to grow up into maturity with God's new nature at work in us. A new nature can only work as **you** allow God to change you.

God did not bury you; He planted you.

WILL I SURVIVE?

Therefore, if anyone is in Christ, he is a new creation; old things have passed away; behold, all things have become new. 2 Corinthians 5:17

As the church, we are living in the most unique time we have ever seen. It's hard to see beyond our circumstances to the big picture when we are focused on what is in front of us. As a result, we can become discouraged with our immediate circumstances. We must stop long enough to pray in the night, and be still long enough to listen in the middle of the day. We must stop and feel after the Lord and let Him show us what He is doing in the earth.

To Nicodemus, Jesus said, unless you are born again, you will not see the kingdom of God (John 3:3). The reason some have been in such a state of confusion and frustration is because we cannot see the Kingdom of God. You may have been born again, but you must die daily to your expectations, desires and wants in order to see what is happening in the Kingdom around you.

What God wants to give is true sight, spiritual sight. When we see what is going on in the spirit-world from God's perspective, we'll have such peace and the things happening in the natural world around us won't bother us anymore. We will have faith in God.

It is not what happens to you that causes you to grow; it is how you respond to what happens to you that causes growth.

2
THE PURPOSE & PROCESS

There is nothing like the aroma of walking into the house after Mother had just baked ten or twelve loaves of bread. Coming from a rather large family, her bread-making was a common occurrence. Just looking at those lightly golden brown loaves cooling on the counter was enough to get any mouth watering.

As the loaves cooled we would wait as long as we could before attempting to take a slice. There was a trick to slicing a nice piece of bread without squashing the whole fresh loaf in the process.

The bread was still warm, and it was so tasty. It didn't need much on it, perhaps some butter, maybe a little homemade strawberry or apricot jam. If a few siblings were in the vicinity, and they always were, a loaf would be gone in a matter of minutes!

The Bread

The Bible draws a parallel between bread and the body of Jesus. Most are familiar with the Scriptural ordinance or sacrament called communion, also known as the Last

WILL I SURVIVE?

Supper or the Lord's Supper. It's the Christian practice of remembering the sacrifice Jesus made when He offered Himself as the propitiation for our sins (1 John 2:2).

The bread symbolized Jesus' body broken, and the wine symbolized His shed blood. We know that in less than 24 hours after the Last Supper, Jesus' body was sacrificed on the cross.

> *And as they were eating, Jesus took bread, blessed and broke it, and gave it to the disciples and said, "Take, eat; this is My body." Then He took the cup, and gave thanks, and gave it to them, saying, "Drink from it, all of you. For this is My blood of the new covenant, which is shed for many for the remission of sins.*
> **Matthew 26:27-28**

In harmony with the intent of this book, we will focus on only part of the sacrament: the bread. Symbolically, Jesus made the parallel between bread and His body with the statement, *"This is My body."* I need to interject here and make it very clear, I do **not** believe in transubstantiation: the belief that the bread and wine are not merely a sign or symbol, but in reality become the actual body and blood of Jesus. Transubstantiation is unbiblical. Jesus only used the bread and wine as symbols to illustrate His coming sacrifice.

Not only is there a Biblical correlation between bread and the body of Jesus, but there is also one between bread and the church. The church of the living God is called

THE PURPOSE & PROCESS

the body of Christ, as well as "one bread."

> *Now you are the body of Christ, and members individually.*
> **1 Corinthians 12:27**

> *The cup of blessing which we bless, is it not the communion of the blood of Christ? The bread which we break, is it not the communion of the body of Christ? For we, though many, are one bread and one body; for we all partake of that one bread.*
> **1 Corinthians 10:16-17**

The Key

Keeping the Biblical bread references in mind, the steps used in making bread in the natural are very similar to the spiritual process of developing the church, Christ's "body." Taking the time to understand bread-making brings great appreciation and peace while contemplating God's purpose and process in your life. Keeping the process in mind will help you see the bigger and broader picture of life.

As you read, **you will** find yourself somewhere in the process. The light of revelation will come and pierce the dark clouds surrounding your understanding of life's purpose. Knowledge will bring comfort and courage to continue on in the process. When you know where you

WILL I SURVIVE?

are now, you can better understand where you need to go, and what it's going to take for you to get there.

In this section, examine with me the comparison Jesus makes between bread and His body. In the last section of this book, I will bring a slightly different practical application. There I will offer further life revelations that will bring aid and comfort through your spiritual, mental and emotional journey. I will attempt to bring you to a place of understanding, and offer tools that will aid in coping with life situations.

Another World

What we call life here and now is, in reality, only a womb compared to eternity. What is 70 or 80 years in light of all eternity? Our life here is a place of transition before we spend eternity elsewhere.

The physical body forms in the womb. There are eyes that do not see, a mouth that does not speak, and hands and feet that are not used, other than to torment their mother. Everything going on in the womb is for the explicit purpose of preparing the human for the next stage of life. In a very short nine months, we go from two cells to a complete human being, comprised of billions of cells. The change is astronomical. A short nine-month cataclysmic alteration takes place just to prepare us for entrance into "another world."

Even so, our time in this world is a preparation place for the entrance into another eternal world, after what we

THE PURPOSE & PROCESS

Preparation

Holiness is a qualifying factor to see the Lord. Holiness comes by purification as our fallen nature is transformed and replaced by God's nature. The process of becoming holy is called sanctification, and it centers on being set apart from everything unholy in order to be dedicated wholly to the Lord. Holiness through sanctification is the will of God for His people.

> **Pursue peace with all people, and holiness, without which no one will see the Lord...**
> **Hebrews 12:14**

Therefore, the purpose of life is for you and I to freely and deliberately choose to say "no" to our own fallen nature and its ways, and choose to say "yes" to God's nature and His ways. Paul explains in this key scripture how the process works:

> **For this is the will of God, your sanctification...**
> **1 Thessalonians 4:3**

*That you **put off**, concerning your former conduct, the old man which grows corrupt according to the deceitful lusts, and be renewed in the spirit of your mind and that you **put on** the new man which was created according to God, in true righteousness and holiness.*
Ephesians 4:22-24

In order for you to be "holy unto the Lord" and part of the "body of Christ" you must "put off" your old human nature. That is, put off your old behavior and character, and "put on" Christ's nature. How do you do this? Verse 23 explains it is by renewing or renovating your mind. You must change your thinking, which in turn changes your actions and conduct to please the Lord Jesus.

Holiness is not a task to complete with mere human grit. In fact, trying to make ourselves holy would indeed be grueling and impossible. You would need rules and regulations, and your life would be a difficult hardship to say the least. Thankfully, God doesn't expect us to become holy in and of ourselves. God gives us His Spirit to help with the sanctification process. We begin the sanctification process by being born again from above, by a water and Spirit birth.

> *However, when He, the Spirit of truth, has come, He will guide you into all truth; for He will not speak on His own authority, but whatever He hears He will speak; and He will tell you things to come.*
> **John 16:13**
>
> *Jesus answered, "Most assuredly, I say to you, unless one is born of water and the Spirit, he cannot enter the kingdom of God.*
> **John 3:5**

Grace

Let me very clear here. I am not talking about working

THE PURPOSE & PROCESS

our way to Heaven. We are without a doubt, saved by God's grace, His enabling power (Ephesians 2:8-9). It is God who gives us the ability, strength and opportunity every day to choose His ways.

Meanwhile, the enemy of your soul walks about seeking whom he may devour (1 Peter 5:8). Your very real adversary wants to get you off track and away from the highway of holiness, which leads to godliness.

A highway shall be there, and a road, And it shall be called the Highway of Holiness. The unclean shall not pass over it, But it shall be for others. Whoever walks the road, although a fool, Shall not go astray.
Isaiah 35:8

Just as a fetus prepares to be born into this world, so we must, with the grace and help of the Lord, prepare ourselves to enter through Heaven's door and be with our Heavenly Father.

If you choose to prepare yourself in this life, you will receive a Heavenly reward in the next life (Matthew 25:32). In Heaven, your perspective will have totally changed, for you will be transformed. You will understand some chose not to qualify themselves and allow the process in life to prepare them. Otherwise how can there be peace and joy in Heaven when somewhere beyond, in outer darkness, there is a lake of fire?

Saved by grace

WILL I SURVIVE?

Life Here is a Womb

Our life here is but a womb. It's a preparation place for us to grow in grace and develop qualities of character and integrity. It's a place to allow the manifestation of the Spirit of our Heavenly Father to shine into the world around us.

Just like a developing fetus, the more you grow and become like your Savior here in this world, the more confined and restrictive you are going to feel. What others may do, you may not. You will live and act differently. Your behavior is not based on fleshly desires.

Though temporarily trapped in this world, you are on the brink of Heaven. You'll be ready to be birthed into eternity. Isn't that legalistic? No. You and I freely and deliberately choose to allow the process of becoming Christ-like to take place in our lives. Like the old-time song says, *"This world is not my home, I'm just a-passing through. My treasures are laid up, somewhere beyond the blue. The angels beckon me from Heaven's open door, and I can't feel at home in this world anymore..."*

Think about the birthing process from a baby's perspective. Let's do a quick interview.

So how are you feeling?

I feel so cramped and uncomfortable. It's like I don't belong here.

THE PURPOSE & PROCESS

What do you mean you don't belong?

I don't know what I mean. I mean I use to have all kinds of freedom to do whatever I wanted to do, but now I'm feeling very restricted. I'm a little nervous here. I feel like something is about to happen.

What's happening?

I've never felt this before. I feel like I'm being pushed forward and there's nothing there, except for darkness. I'm scared. I don't want to leave here. I've never been anywhere else. This is all I know. I don't know what's out there.

Where do you think you might be going?

I think I'm dying.

Dying? That sounds terrible. Are you ready?

NO! I don't want to die. I've never died before. All I see is darkness and I think death is just beyond that very small area. Somehow I think I may have to go through there. And I know that is not going to be very comfortable. I know I'm not going to like that, no, not at all!

You and I can see the humor here, but the baby

WILL I SURVIVE?

doesn't! We understand the purpose of pregnancy and how the birthing process works. It is critical the baby be born on time. It is birth to us, but from the baby's perspective it is death. It is quite literally, a whole new and very different world for the infant, and that can be a very frightening thing.

Choose Life

With the revelation of the purpose and process in life, you can endure pain and tears, for you know there will be great joy after it's all over. This life here is not the end, but only the preparation ground for something new to begin.

> *For to me to live is Christ, and to die is gain.*
> **Philippians 1:21**

> *. . . I take pleasure in infirmities, in reproaches, in needs, in persecutions, in distresses, for Christ's sake. For when I am weak, then I am strong.*
> **2 Corinthians 12:10**

When you have an understanding of the purpose, you can face and go through difficulties. If you can find meaning in the process you will not only survive, but you will thrive. Keep allowing yourself to become better, not bitter. The old nature is dying and a new nature is being born and growing within. With dying, there will be pain.

THE PURPOSE & PROCESS

It seldom comes easy.

Tribulation is Part of the Process

Patience is good, and I want it now! I shall always remember someone telling me, "Never pray for patience." The Bible says tribulation produces patience (Romans 5:3). Therefore if you pray for patience, you are asking for tribulation. As much as I would like to have the quality of patience, who in their right mind would ask for tribulation?

In order to die, or be birthed into new life, there is going to be some pain.

What Luke 21:19 is saying is, "in your cheerful endurance you will preserve your life." The root meaning of patience here gives the idea of being crowded and burdened with anguish and affliction. Don't give up, or give in to anguish and affliction. Don't yield to calamity, but bear-up under it, for those who endure and do not abort the process, shall be saved (Matthew 24:13).

Wait on the LORD: be of good courage, and he shall strengthen your heart: wait, I say, on the LORD. **Psalms 27:14**

In your patience possess your souls.
Luke 21:19

You therefore must endure hardship as a good soldier of Jesus Christ. **2 Timothy 2:3**

WILL I SURVIVE?

Pain With Purpose

Pain is a by-product of growth and healing. Take surgery for example. The surgeon cuts and in fact "hurts" us. We allow him to perform the surgery, knowing we will spend days, or weeks in recovery. The pain is very real. We hurt. I'm sure you could tell a few stories of doctor visits or hospital stays, yet because of your understanding of the purpose of surgery, you endure the process in the midst of hurt and pain.

In life, some people may intentionally mean us harm. Others inadvertently hurt us. Either way, pain presents an opportunity. There is a higher purpose at work. You can choose to allow the Lord to form you into His image through the situation. You can use the bad hand dealt to you as a stepping-stone, not a stumbling block. You can accept the bread-making process and become His body, preparing for another world: Heaven.

> **Harm is pain without purpose, the devil's territory. The wounds are senseless, needless and there is no redeeming value.**

The difference between hurt and harm is purpose. Situations will always arise in your life that require you to make a choice. Crisis is nothing but short-term pain for long-term gain. With revelation of the bread-making process, you will begin to associate struggle with a higher purpose for your spiritual, mental and emotional health and growth.

THE PURPOSE & PROCESS

Christ Being Formed

The Apostle Paul cast a vision and gave purpose using the analogy of travailing and laboring in childbirth. Just as there are pains in the natural birthing process, there are painful experiences in life as you are conformed into the image of Christ Jesus.

Take a walk down the halls of a maternity ward. Some of the sounds you hear will send chills down your spine, yet no one is calling 911. No one is panicking, except perhaps a first time father. Why? Because everyone knows, pain is a part of the process of giving birth. It's expected. It's what's going to happen every time. In the process of time, all things being equal, eventually tears of joy and congratulations will come.

My little children, of whom I travail in birth again until Christ be formed in you...
Galatians 4:19

There is a purpose in every life situation. The Lord God is not willing that any should perish (2 Peter 3:9), and there stands an open invitation to all to be born again (John 3:5). As the natural child grows up to becoming like it's parents, the true child of God will conform and be made into Christ's image. We reflect the image of our Heavenly Father. If you want to make Heaven your home, you and I are going to go through a process. Look at the words used to describe our prime example, Jesus Christ.

WILL I SURVIVE?

Who, in the days of His flesh, when He had offered up prayers and supplications, with vehement cries and tears to Him who was able to save Him from death, and was heard because of His godly fear, though He was a Son, **yet He learned obedience by the things which He suffered.** *And having been perfected, He became the author of eternal salvation to all who obey Him…*
Hebrews 5:7-9

You mean Jesus had to learn obedience through suffering? Does that mean I may have to "suffer" a few things in order for me to learn some things? If you are in the will of God, shouldn't everything go smoothly? Jesus' learning ended with this summation statement in His garden:

…Saying, "Father, if it is Your will, take this cup away from Me; **nevertheless not My will, but Yours, be done."** *Then an angel appeared to Him from heaven, strengthening Him.*
Luke 22:42-43

What a profound, powerful and liberating statement: "Not my will, but thine, be done." How long will you wait before you honestly and sincerely make the same declaration?

THE PURPOSE & PROCESS

The Bottom Line

Being born again of water and Spirit is the beginning of the creative process. The ultimate goal is to be changed into the image of **Jesus Christ**. I encourage you to embrace the necessary first step of surviving the process. Accept God's purpose in your life, and allow the breadmaking process of becoming His body. If you allow the whole process to unfold it will finish with your natural death, which of course, from eternity's perspective, is a birth into true life.

The creative process we call life on earth is only a womb preparing us for real life, eternal life, which begins at what we call death. The end of a pregnancy is the beginning of a whole new being we call a baby. Just the same, our human natural death is also the beginning of a whole new being, the entrance to eternal life in a whole new realm.

BREAD-MAKING

3
SOWING

In order to make bread you need dough, which comes from flour. Flour comes from wheat, and initially you can only get wheat if you plant it. So, the first step in the bread making process is sowing. You have to plant the seed.

The Four Types of Hearers

The sower went out to sow. The parable in Matthew 13, often referred to as the Parable of the Sower, is in reality a parable about four different types of soils, which represent four different types of souls. The Seed, God's Word and love, is constantly sowed to us all. The difference between us isn't in how much of God's Word and love we have access to, but it is in how we receive what is sown into our hearts.

> **How you hear and respond to the Word and Spirit of God will determine your outcome in the process of life.**

The four different types of soil represent differing

WILL I SURVIVE?

receptivity to the Word of God. When the Spirit of God begins His work and the process of transformation in your life, you will respond in one of four ways. The revelatory question becomes, which type of hearer are you? You **will** fall into one of the categories. How you hear and respond to the Word and Spirit of God will determine your outcome in the process of life.

First there is the "wayside" soil, which represents the **"Hard-Hearted Hearer."** This person is very superficial in regard to God.

> *When anyone hears the word of the kingdom, and does not understand it, then the wicked one comes and snatches away what was sown in his heart. This is he who received seed by the wayside.*
> **Matthew 13:19**

God wants to speak; however we are not listening. Even if we do hear from God, we do not allow the Word of God to drop into our heart and spirit. The Word of the Lord simply rolls away like water off a duck's back.

What would God have to do to get your attention? What if God is trying to get your attention through life's problems and predicaments? How many times do you need to go around the same mountain to reach your destination?

I remember a young lady who, for a short time, attended the church I pastored. The Spirit of God was so powerful in the service, and there she sat. It was as if

SOWING

the Word of God would just bounce off of her. Nothing seemed to penetrate past her glassy eyes. It's wasn't long before she was gone.

Secondly, there is the "stony place" type of soil, which represents the **"Hollow-Hearted Hearer."** This person not only hears the Word of God, but receives it! The problem here is the individual has no strength of character to endure hardship. The moment there is some difficulty in life, they bail on living for God.

> *But he who received the seed on stony places, this is he who hears the word and immediately receives it with joy; yet he has no root in himself, but endures only for a while. For when tribulation, or persecution arises because of the word, immediately he stumbles.*
> ***Matthew 13:20-21***

Are you in church for a good time, or a long time? Does everything have to be a "spiritual high" for you? Or do you have a depth of commitment? Some people still have the world's "party" spirit in them, and need to be stimulated all the time. When real life happens, they can't handle it and instead they move on to the next big thing that will entertain them.

You will find yourself a "Hollow-Hearted Hearer" if you struggle against God when He wants to interject and speak change into your life. For you, church is a social meeting place and a way to ease the conscience.

The third type of soil is the "thorny place," the **"Half-**

WILL I SURVIVE?

Hearted Hearer." I find this type of person interesting. The Bible does not say this person does not love the Lord. No doubt he does. It's just that his priorities are off; everything else comes before his relationship and commitment to Jesus. He is just so busy with life now, he is sidetracked from thinking of eternity.

> *Now he who received seed among the thorns is he who hears the word, and the cares of this world and the deceitfulness of riches choke the word, and he becomes unfruitful.*
> **Matthew 13:22**

It is hard to think of just one person when it comes to the "thorny place" type of soil. I've seen it far too many times. I know you love the Lord, or you wouldn't be reading this book, but does everything seem to come before your relationship with Jesus?

Be truthful. Stop and evaluate your last six months. When "something" comes up, do you miss church? When was the last time you actually sat down and read your Bible? Can you talk to Jesus for longer than seven minutes? Isn't it easier to just watch TV? Jesus is important to you, but not as important as other things in your life.

Salvation may be free, but discipleship will cost you everything.

Let's take a look at the scriptures. The Book of James is all about reality. If faith saves, it also works. The

SOWING

reformist, Martin Luther, despised the Book of James and tried to get it thrown out of the Bible. Luther was a theologian consumed with justification by faith. James was more of a practical man. He said if you are saved, then show me the evidence of it.

> *Do not merely listen to the word, and so deceive yourselves. Do what it says.*
> ***James 1:22 NIV***

> *What good is it, my brothers, if a man claims to have faith but has no deeds? Can such faith save him?*
> ***James 2:14 NIV***

> *In the same way, faith by itself, if it is not accompanied by action, is dead.*
> ***James 2:17 NIV***

A relationship with Jesus takes time and commitment, which is not restricted to Sunday morning. There is far more to being a Christian than just saying one prayer, way back when.

Finally, the "good ground" represents the **"Honest Hearted Hearer."** Not only does this person hear and receive the Word, but he grows in the process of maturity. He allows Christ to be formed in him. As a result, he becomes fruitful. The Lord Jesus' mission becomes his mission (Luke 19:10).

WILL I SURVIVE?

But he who received seed on the good ground is he who hears the word and understands it, who indeed bears fruit and produces: some a hundredfold, some sixty, some thirty.
Matthew 13:23

Stones

In my travels to Israel, I gained insight as to why people in the Middle East practiced stoning as corporal punishment in Bible days. Stones are literally everywhere. You do not have to go out to find a stone, simply bend your knee and retrieve one!

If you are going to grow wheat on the stony ground in Israel, you have to remove all of the stones. This applies to our lives as hearers; we need to dig out the "stones" from our heart, which keep the Word from gaining the depth it needs to grow. Without growth, there will be no fruit.

Without growth, there will be no fruit.

The lack of fruit is an indication that there are too many stones in our lives. The seed is not able to go deep enough for it to grow and mature. To be effective, before we put seed in we first need to take stones out.

You may have read or heard this illustration before, but it's worth repeating. The origin of the story is unknown, and there are different variations of it out there. It's the story of coffee and the mayonnaise jar. It goes something

SOWING

like this:

In front of his philosophy class, a professor picked up a very large and empty mayonnaise jar and proceeded to fill it with golf balls. Then he asked the students if the jar was full. They agreed; it was full.

The professor then picked up a box of pebbles and poured them into the jar. He shook the jar slightly and the pebbles dropped into the open spaces between the golf balls. He asked his students again if the jar was full. They agreed it was.

Next, the professor picked up a box of sand and poured it into the jar. Of course, the sand filled up everything else. He asked once more if the jar was full. The students responded unanimously, "Yes."

The professor then produced two cups of coffee from under the table and poured them into the jar, effectively filling the empty space between the sand. The students laughed.

After the laughter subsided, the professor commented, "I want you to recognize this jar represents your life. The golf balls are the important things: God, family, your children, your health, friends, and your favorite pastimes. Thus, if everything else were lost and only they remained, your life would still be full.

"The pebbles are the other things that matter, like your job, your house and your car. The sand is everything else, all the small stuff. If you put the sand into the jar first," he continued, "there is no room for the pebbles or the golf balls.

WILL I SURVIVE?

"The same goes for life. If you spend all your time and energy on the small stuff, you will never have room for the things that are important to you. Pay attention to the things that are critical to your happiness."

One of the students raised her hand and inquired what the coffee represented.

The professor smiled. "I'm glad you asked. It just goes to show you that no matter how full your life may seem, there's always room for a couple of cups of coffee with a friend."

The most important and valued things in life should always be first.

The first step in the process of becoming bread is emptying yourself of as much of the wrong stuff as possible. This cleaning out allows God the opportunity to put the good stuff and right stuff in us, in the right order. Remember, you always have a choice. You can resist and fight the process, or you can be teachable and grow in the hands of God.

The Ground Determines the Results

My only mission as a pulpit preacher is to be faithful in listening to what God wants me to say and to say it! I have repeatedly said, "It's not a matter of 'if' I say something you will take offence with, it is a matter of 'when.' If I

...Work out your own salvation with fear and trembling. Philippians 2:12

SOWING

am speaking as an oracle of God, and God is Holy and man is sinful, then at some point in time I'm going to say something you may not like."

You and I are to speak truth in love (Ephesians 4:15). At the same time, we are to speak the truth without fear, or favor of men. Sadly and very unfortunately, many pulpits seem far too concerned with political and religious correctness.

I would rather risk you being upset with me here and now, with the chance to right yourself, then you being upset and offended in eternity where there is no possibility of repentance and correcting your ways.

Be ready in season and out of season. Convince, rebuke, exhort, with all longsuffering and teaching. For the time will come when they will not endure sound doctrine, but according to their own desires, because they have itching ears, they will heap up for themselves teachers; and they will turn their ears away from the truth, and be turned aside to fables. But you be watchful in all things, endure afflictions... **2 Timothy 4:2-5**

The seed, or the Word of God, goes forth to whom-soever. As conviction pricks the heart, one person humbles their self under the mighty hand of God. Another takes offence and walks away. We all have a choice, but in the process of time our soil will either allow the seed to grow,

WILL I SURVIVE?

or will choke it out.

> *...[The Heavenly Father] makes His sun rise on the evil and on the good, and sends rain on the just and on the unjust.*
> **Matthew 5:45**

Reality check here: you and I cannot make seed grow. As much as we would like to, we cannot force someone to turn to God. Nor can we make someone accept and embrace the process. What we can do, is water the seed with the tears in prayer.

Prayer Changes Things

Prayer moves the hand of God. Prayer doesn't force God's hand, or tell Him what to do. Yet through prayer, we can intercede on behalf of others. We can ask God to have mercy, to intervene and allow His grace and Spirit to touch and move on our friends and loved ones.

> *He who continually goes forth weeping, bearing seed for sowing, shall doubtless come again with rejoicing, bringing his sheaves with him.*
> **Psalm 126:6**

You cannot reap what is not planted. It is the law of nature. You cannot have a harvest, unless seed is sown. If someone does not sow seed, there will be nothing to

SOWING

harvest. There will be no wheat to make flour, to turn into dough, to bake into bread.

But this I say: He who sows sparingly will also reap sparingly, and he who sows bountifully will also reap bountifully.
2 Corinthians 9:6

You and I have the choice to submit to God and His ways. You may choose to go around the mountain time and again, remaining stuck in a rut or holding pattern. Your choices may keep you bound for a few months, or a few years. But God's laws are immutable. His purpose and process will remain until the end of time.

That at the name of Jesus every knee should bow, of those in heaven, and of those on earth, and of those under the earth, and that every tongue should confess that Jesus Christ is Lord...
Philippians 2:10-11

Tares

Inevitably, tares will grow up among wheat. The funny thing about tares is that they look like wheat, until near harvest time. So why not get rid of the tares, those who have the appearance of being a follower of Jesus? Answer: removing a tare is not worth possibly losing good wheat. The Bible gives very clear instruction that the wheat and the tares are to grow up together until harvest (Matthew 13:29-30).

The seed is sown. Slowly, as we approach harvest season, something begins to happen. The tares stand up straight. Almost in a defiant act of rebellion, their stature says, "I will not be moved. I will not bend to the purpose, nor bow to the process of God."

In contrast, the wheat bows over, ripe with harvest grain. This represents people who humble and submit themselves to God's process, and allows Christ to be formed in them. They allow the hard knocks in life to work away the rough edges of bitterness, resentment and unforgiveness. They willingly choose to let go of their natural carnal nature and let the nature of the Spirit of God dwell and grow in them.

Harvest time is the only time you can tell the difference between wheat and tares. When the Spirit of conviction begins to move, the wheat begins to bow, and the tares expose themselves as they stand tall in insolence to God. Now you can begin to remove the tares as you walk through the ripened field (Matthew 13:30).

I will elaborate further on the role and power of conviction in the next chapter. Suffice it to say, without conviction, you will not be saved.

Two Men

Here's a story of two men. Let's call the first man Randy. Randy was raised around church, though he was never

SOWING

really committed. He was the likeable type, high-spirited. He started attending the church where I was Pastor and shortly thereafter, sincerely submitted to God and was born again.

It wasn't long before Randy's strong will and personality manifested itself. I would give direction, and regardless of what the instruction concerned, somehow Randy never seemed to like or agree with it.

Without conviction, you will not be saved.

Don't get me wrong; Randy was a nice guy. I liked him. Yet I knew that if he did not surrender and submit his strong-willed character to God, at some point down the road it would lead him away, out of the purpose of God.

Then it happened. Randy rose up in insubordination. I remember standing with him, explaining God's purpose and our need to allow the Lord to consecrate all areas of our personality to His will and character. I spoke almost nose to nose, rather directly, with great care and love in my voice and heart.

To my pleasant relief, he thanked me for standing up to him and speaking so candidly with him. "No one has ever spoken to me like that before," he said. "Thank you for caring for me enough to talk to me. I imagine that was difficult for you, but I needed it."

Randy's life changed that day. He stepped into and allowed the process of God to change him into the image of Jesus. He has thanked me and conveyed his story to many new church goers, in hopes of helping

WILL I SURVIVE?

them submit to the hand of God in their lives. Randy and his wife are leaders in the church they now attend. Their son is in ministry and their daughter is going to marry a missionary.

Then there was the second man, Eric. He said he was called to ministry. Eric had difficult experiences in the church where he was from. He decided I had more to offer him and could help him into ministry, so he changed churches.

My ministerial philosophy is everyone who comes through the doors is a potential leader. I do not qualify you. You will qualify or disqualify yourself, in time.

It seemed as if Eric always had an axe to grind with people. Everything was difficult for him. One day, while doing work around the church, Eric blew up with anger again. I attempted to talk with him, but he wanted nothing of it. Finally, while standing outside the front doors of the church I asked him this question; "Eric, are you at all teachable?"

Eric leaned towards me, cocked his head to one side and replied, "I guess I'm not." Sadly, my last words to him were, "Then I guess there's nothing I can do for you."

SOWING

God resists the proud, But gives grace to the humble. Therefore humble yourselves under the mighty hand of God, that He may exalt you in due time.
1 Peter 5:5-6

I have long determined and settled in my heart, when God speaks, my answer will always be, "Yes Lord." Sometimes it may take me a couple of minutes. On the odd occasion, it's taken me several days to work past my human nature. But my answer will always be, "Yes, Lord."

The greatest oxymoron in the religious world is to say, "No, Lord." It is fundamentally impossibility to put a 'No' with 'Lord.' If Jesus is Lord, your Lord, who are you to say no?

But why do you call Me 'Lord, Lord,' and not do the things which I say?
Luke 6:46

If you are teachable, you are fixable.

4
REAPING

The sun shined its rays onto the field below. At other times, the rain dropped from clouds looming high above, and watered the ground. Over time, wheat grew. Growth comes through the natural progression of life. Growth is life. If we are not growing, we are dying. Everything growing moves. It may be a very slow movement, but if there is growth, there is movement. With movement comes friction, and with friction usually comes a little pain.

If we are not growing, we are dying.

The wheat is fully grown, and it's time for the harvest. A harvest is cut down using a sickle. The sickle is the Word of God, and the Word of God can cut.

For the word of God is living and powerful, and sharper than any two-edged sword, piercing even to the division of soul and spirit, and of joints and marrow, and is a discerner of the thoughts and intents of the heart.
Hebrews 4:12

WILL I SURVIVE?

We may go a little outside of your comfort zone here. Sometimes as the Almighty speaks into your mortal life, the Word of God does make you feel uncomfortable. Anyone who comes face to face, with the Almighty God ought to feel uncomfortable, just a little. I'm talking about a feeling you have when you know God is talking to you about some things that need to change. The feeling is called conviction, and conviction cuts.

Conviction

Conviction is an interesting emotion. Today's society does not like to be inconvenienced or feel uncomfortable, which happens as the Spirit of God cuts through defensive walls and pierces the heart. It can be a very awkward and difficult place. You have two choices in your response to conviction. Humble yourself and submit to God, or harden your heart and run. What will you choose?

I remember teaching a number of home Bible studies to a young man. For the sake of this story, I'll call him Lance. He seemed to drink up the Good News at first. Then conviction began to set in as the Spirit of God began to speak concerning specific areas of his life.

Lance dropped by the church one day to cancel all further Bible studies. He mumbled out his excuses. I interjected. "You're just feeling too much conviction aren't you? And the Spirt of God wants you to make some changes that you really don't want to? Isn't that about it?" I asked.

REAPING

He nodded his head, made a few more comments about his friends and walked away. There is no one more miserable than the person who is feeling the touch and conviction of God on their life, and yet still refuses to listen.

God is holy. Mankind, due to his fallen nature, is sinful. As the Spirit of God moves upon you with conviction and begins to reveal areas that are not pleasing to Him, it will feel uncomfortable. The little bit of discomfort grabs our attention. We can listen to God, and if we correct the area He is convicting us over, we will have peace and the blessings of God.

Sometimes conviction can be confused with condemnation. Conviction says you have "done" wrong, whereas condemnation says you "are" wrong. Conviction brings hope: "I will forgive if you repent." Condemnation brings discouragement, depression and feelings of hopelessness.

Azusa

I want to share a prophetic utterance given and written down over 100 years ago, which is still applicable and revelatory for us today. The prophecy occurred at what is called the great Azusa Street Revival.

"In the last days three things will happen in the great Pentecostal movement. There will be an overemphasis on power, rather than on righteousness. There will be an

WILL I SURVIVE?

overemphasis on praise, to a God they no longer pray to. There will be an overemphasis on the gifts of the Spirit, rather than on the Lordship of Christ."

Does that not describe our church world today? So much could be said on these three utterances. Suffice it to say, there is a vast difference between confessing Jesus as Lord and making Jesus, Lord of your life. Equally, there is a vast difference between confession and repentance. In God's great love and mercy, He tells us that if we acknowledge and confess our sins He will forgive (1 John 1:9).

By definition, repentance is a 180-degree turn around. It's changing to go in the exact opposite direction than you were headed before. A truly repentant person makes a complete and total change in their life. Not understanding the difference between repentance and confession is one of the main reasons there is great confusion in today's church world.

> **There is a vast difference between confessing Jesus as Lord, and making Jesus, Lord.**

We have far too many churchgoers who have not repented. They confess they are sinners, but their life has not completely and totally changed, at least not to the extent the Lord desires and requires in His Word. It's almost as if church services are religious club meetings every Sunday. Get it over with quickly and conveniently, and then you're on your way with your day and life. No wonder the world mocks our hypocrisy. It's no surprise

REAPING

there is great spiritual confusion in our world.

It is an indictment against the church, when the church can feel comfortable in the sinful world and sin can feel comfortable in the church. All throughout scripture there was to be a separation and distinction between the people of God and the world. Nowadays, there is such a blending and blurring, it's hard to distinguish a believer from a non-believer.

It wasn't too long ago when you could take a survey on the street and the "heathen" could make a list of do's and don'ts of church-going Christians. To a great extent, today the lines of separation are gone. I remember when Sunday was considered the "Lord's Day" and very few people would work. Those who did work only worked out of necessity. It was a day of rest, a day off to spend with family and friends. To miss a church service was unheard of unless you were dying!

Jesus put it in perspective when He asked the question we read in Luke 6:46. In our modern vernacular He is saying, "Hello?! What you are doing speaks so loud that I can't hear a word you are saying."

**What you are doing speaks so loud,
I can't hear a word you are saying.**

"But why do you call Me 'Lord, Lord,' and not do the things which I say? Whoever comes to Me, and hears My sayings and does them, I will show you whom he is like: He is like a man building a house, who dug deep and laid the foundation on the rock. And

WILL I SURVIVE?

when the flood arose, the stream beat vehemently against that house, and could not shake it, for it was founded on the rock. But he who heard and did nothing is like a man who built a house on the earth without a foundation, against which the stream beat vehemently; and immediately it fell. And the ruin of that house was great."
Luke 6:46-49

Where is conviction in our churches today? When is the last time you kind of felt a little "uncomfortable" in church as a result of the power and presence of God convicting you? Or should I ask, when was the last time you felt as if God were talking to you and asking you to make changes in your life? How did you respond?

Welcome, But Not Comfortable

Again, please do not misunderstand my point here. I want people to feel invited and very much welcomed in church. I want everyone to feel the warmth of God's love and acceptance. However there is a difference between feeling welcomed and feeling spiritually "comfortable." I want you to come face to face with the Living God. And if you do, how can you leave His presence and just feel comfortable, without a challenge to grow and change?

Many, many years ago, an elderly woman of God shared a dream she had. Her dream impacted and shook me to the core. I will never forget it. In this dream there

REAPING

were masses of people who were so very angry with a few men. The mass of people were yelling at and beating up the men. Finally, the mob put a rope around the men and hung them dead.

The godly woman was horrified and disturbed by the scene. With a troubled heart she asked the Lord, "Jesus, who are these men? What terrible things did they do to deserve such treatment?"

Then the Lord spoke revelation to this dear Sister, "These are Pastors and the people are the congregations of their churches."

> **It is an indictment against the church when the church can feel comfortable in the sinful world, and sin can feel comfortable in the church.**

"Oh my," gasped the Sister, "Why are the people so angry?" she inquired.

The answer came back, "The people are angry because they missed My second coming. And now they are taking their animosity and frustration out on the Shepherds who did not tell them the truth."

Lord Jesus, have mercy on the men, women, boys and girls who do not have a preacher with enough courage and strength to boldly proclaim truth.

For the time will come when they will not endure sound doctrine, but according to their own desires, because they have itching ears, they will heap up for themselves teachers; and they will turn their ears

WILL I SURVIVE?

away from the truth, and be turned aside to fables.
2 Timothy 4:3-4

Man, or woman of God, you have a divine appointment and responsibility before God to speak truth. If there was ever a time that we need to hear a clear and certain sound, it is today. All roads do not lead to heaven. There is only one road and only one way to be saved. Jesus is the only answer for the world today.

Still, speaking truth does not give us permission to be rude or mean-spirited. We must speak truth in love with compassion. God is love and the idea is to speak and direct people to Him with love and respect.

But, speaking the truth in love, may grow up into Him in all things, which is the head, even Christ.
Ephesians 4:15

Revivals of the Past

> Jesus is the only answer for the world today.

The great revivals of the past were revivals of conviction. The Azusa Street Revival changed the religious landscape and became the most vibrant force for world evangelism in the 20th century. As people simply walked past the outside of the old mission where the revival was, they would fall to their knees under conviction of the Spirit of God.

One night during the great Welsh Revival, God's

REAPING

Spirit of conviction touched the hearts of a small valley town. People would awake from sleep, and get out of their beds to pray and seek God. Whole communities were turned upside down. Though no official records were kept, historians conservatively estimated 150,000 people turned to God in repentance through that revival. The crime rate dropped to next to nothing as people awoke to the fear of God.

Charles Finny Revivals were always characterized by great conviction. So much so that bars would close because they were empty. Everyone was going to the revival. Here's a quote from Finny's journal: "The congregation began to fall from their seats, and they fell in every direction, and cried for mercy. If I had a sword in each hand I could not have cut them off their seats as fast as they fell."

Conviction, truly, is a gift from God. To be able to feel the prick of God's Spirit touching your heart, calling, asking you to make yourself right with the Maker, is a priceless gift. How can you and I turn away from sin and straighten out our lives, aligning to the Word of God, if we first don't feel conviction and the need to change?

Peter, the man with the keys to the Kingdom of Heaven (Matthew 16:19), preached the first New Testament sermon. By doing so, he opened and announced the opportunity for all to be saved in and through the name

Conviction is a gift from God.

WILL I SURVIVE?

of the Lord Jesus.

After Peter proclaimed Jesus was both Lord and Savior, great conviction settled over the crowd. It was not just a feeling, nor was it simply the nodding of the head. It was an inner hunger and desire to repent. Conviction compels you to act and do something based on your belief.

> *Now when they heard this, **they were cut to the heart**, and said to Peter and the rest of the apostles, "Men and brethren, **what shall we do?**" Then Peter said to them, "Repent, and let every one of you be baptized in the name of Jesus Christ for the remission of sins; and you shall receive the gift of the Holy Spirit.*
> **Acts 2:37-38**

Notice the First Church was founded on conviction. They were "cut" to the heart, or convicted in their spirit, and acted accordingly. Without that cutting conviction you will drift in the sea of religious teachings.

> *And in vain they worship Me, Teaching as doctrines the commandments of men.*
> **Matthew 15:9**

Reap the Harvest with Conviction

Conviction is God's Spirit convincing someone of their

REAPING

need to turn their life around and start pleasing God. It is the awakening and submission to the Word of God as the authority in their life.

To have faith in God is to be persuaded or convinced to the point you willing choose to act on your belief. When we fall in line with the Lord's conviction, we will begin to deny our sinful desires. Repentance is the opposite of our societal ideology of "me, myself and I."

Conviction is not about a person trying to persuade or convince you. It is God who takes preaching or teaching and by His Spirit, He convinces and He persuades. Music and other programs and gimmicks are no substitute for good old Holy Spirit conviction.

I'm going step out and say people who are not drawn by conviction to Jesus, will not be able to be pastored. They will resist the pruning shears of the Lord when He begins to prune the dead wood from off their branches (John 15). I will cover this concept more in-depth in the next two chapters.

Let's be transparent. How do you respond to preaching when it starts to challenge you? What do you do when the Spirit of God confronts you, and He requires you to actually change something, do something, to altar some way of private life?

I'll tell what I've seen far too many people do: they balk. They squawk and squirm. Then they "feel led of the Lord" to go to another church where they will start all over, until they are challenged again. Conviction will challenge us. Submission to conviction is called

WILL I SURVIVE?

repentance. Conviction is a dying to self, a surrender of your will and replacing it with God's will.

The only hope for the group who travels from church to church every two to five years is to submit to the conviction of the Holy Spirit and plant themselves into one church.

> **Conviction is a dying to self, a surrender of your will and replacing it with God's will.**

Godly leadership in a person's life is crucial. At the same time, you cannot submit to a teaching just because someone from "church" says so. You and I must get to a place where we choose to live a righteous, holy lifestyle, separate from the world, because we believe it. We must live out our lives based on what God reveals to us about our lifestyles.

If you change only for a person the change won't last. But if the Lord sends conviction and you accept and embrace it, then your conviction will stay with you wherever you are and whomever you're with. That's called conviction.

Sheaves

Once we have plowed and sown the seed, the Lord God waters and causes the wheat to grow. In the harvest, you gather all the ripened wheat together, which are now called sheaves.

God's Spirit moves upon the hearts and souls of men and women, boys and girls. Conviction takes place and

REAPING

the harvester goes forth to reap. What is next in the bread-making process? Well, you bring the harvest, or sheaves, to the threshing floor.

Those who sow in tears SHALL reap in joy. He who continually goes forth weeping, bearing seed for sowing, SHALL doubtless come again with rejoicing, bringing his sheaves with him.
Psalm 126:5-6

Harvesting the sheaves begins another step in separating the wheat from the chaff, which I will cover extensively in the next chapter. At this point, I will, however, share an amazing statistic. Somewhere between 70 and 80 percent of the volume of sheaves is chaff. The Bible calls the chaff "ungodly."

The ungodly are not so, but are like the chaff which the wind drives away.
Psalm 1:4

The ungodly are those who will not "fall in line" or "line up" to the Word of God. The ungodly are not committed to the God's purpose and process. Everything God orchestrates in the life of a believer is intended to find out whether they are chaff or wheat.

Between 70 and 80 percent of the volume of the sheaves is actually chaff. The Bible calls the chaff "ungodly."

WILL I SURVIVE?

Let me share a funny spin on a typical post-revival conversation: "Praise the Lord! We had 14 born again last month."

"How many did you keep?"

"We kept all the wheat. We do not want to keep the chaff!"

Once a person is born again they cannot be unborn. As born-again believers, we are in a completely different dimension than we were before. If we do not allow Christ to be formed in us, and if we indeed abort the process, then we become known as the ungodly. Do you see the difference? An aborted baby is still a baby. A life does not cease to have ever existed simply because it is terminated.

"If the righteous one is scarcely saved, where will the ungodly and the sinner appear?"
1 Peter 4:18

The ungodly will not go to heaven. Not because they are sinners, but because they resisted the purpose and process of God. They did not let go of their nature and allow the nature of God be formed in them.

Though chaff is ungodly it does serve a purpose. Chaff is used to kindle the fire to cook the bread. These are the people who come in under conviction and leave through the process of threshing, winnowing, or sifting.

Every time someone comes to the altar, we do not know if they are chaff or wheat. We do know they are sheaves. We don't put sheaves in the barn. We put wheat

REAPING

in the barn. What do we do with the sheaves, the new converts? We take them to the threshing floor, the altar.

What do most people do with new converts? In our politically and religiously correct society, we tiptoe around them. We don't want to offend anyone. What does God do with new converts? He immediately puts them on the threshing floor to find out if they are wheat or chaff.

When it comes time to find out if they were willing to be part of the bread, the body, conformed into the image of Jesus, they will prove themselves wheat or chaff. If they are chaff, they abort the process and in essence say, "I don't need this. I'm out of here." Wheat, on the other hand, will remain.

I mentioned in the beginning of the book that you will find yourself somewhere in these pages. Have you recognized yourself yet? Has the Lord Jesus revealed more of His purpose and process in your life? The next few chapters address in more detail the difference between wheat and chaff.

> **Everything God orchestrates in the life of a believer is intended to find out whether they are chaff or wheat.**

5
CHAFF

The Threshing, Winnowing and Sifting Process

Harvesting is a huge, exciting undertaking. But bringing in the harvest is only a step in preparing to grind the wheat into flour to make bread. For thousands of years, farmers used a basic, three-part system to prepare wheat grain to the point it could be ground into flour: threshing, winnowing, and sifting. In modern times the process is much easier due to the use of large combines, which work day and night.

Sheaves Are Not Wheat

When we experience a great move of God's Spirit, it is as if a reaper is going forth to harvest. Conviction cuts to the heart, the wheat bows and tares stand tall. The harvest is gathered, but what comes next? The harvesters bring the sheaves to the threshing floor. Is the harvest wheat yet? No. The Bible says it is "sheaves" (Psalms 126:6).

WILL I SURVIVE?

I am told somewhere between 70 and 80 percent of the volume of sheaves is chaff! That sounds so amazing to me. Up to 80 percent of the volume that comes into the farmyard is basic filler and unusable. Well, technically I suppose chaff has a use… You will be astounded when you learn where and how it is used.

The Bible says chaff represents ungodly people. The ungodly are those who will not "line up" to the Word of God. They resist and do not allow the process of Christ to form in them. They are the non-committed, undedicated, socially religious.

Somewhere between 70 and 80 percent of the volume of sheaves is chaff, basic filler and unusable.

The ungodly are not so, But are like the chaff which the wind drives away.
Psalm 1:4

The process has started. Everything God allows to occur from the time a person is saved is intended to find out whether that person is chaff or wheat. Where are you in the process?

You do not receive a pass just because you showed up, raised your hand, or walked down to the altar. The goal is to "endure," to stay under or in faith, despite life's complications until you reach the end. Life's complications are there to allow Christ to form in you.

CHAFF

*And you will be hated by all for My name's sake. But he who endures to the end
will be saved.*
Matthew 10:22

You can't make bread out of chaff, and you do not necessarily want to keep chaff, though it does serve a purpose. The chaff is used to kindle the fire, to cook the bread. Who does the chaff fire represent? Those people who come in the church under conviction and leave through the process of: (1) **threshing**, (2) **winnowing** and (3) **sifting**.

The next chapter explains the chaff fire. Part of the fire comes from chaff "bad-mouthing" wheat. Such situations provide the heat to turn dough into bread. If you stop their mouths from persecution, you put out the fire. No fire; no bread. It's part of the process.

Every time we baptize someone, we really don't know if they are chaff or wheat. We do know they are sheaves. Some of them really did turn to God, and really did repent of their sins. They may have shed tears and felt great sorrow over sin. Just by turning away from sin towards God, they feel better and obtain some relief

You cannot make bread out of chaff.

from the pressure and torment of sin. As time goes on, we will find out if they are willing to be part of the His body, the bread.

Unfortunately, some prove they are not prepared to

go the distance. They won't come out and actually say they don't want to go the distance. Instead, they will drag their feet and resist all of the teachable moments in life.

As a result of not understanding the process of separating chaff from wheat, we discredit many moves of God. Rather than be inspired by what God is doing and rejoicing with all of the sheaves coming in, we dismissed it as not truly genuine. We see many people come into the church, but few stay. As a result, we think, "It must not have been of God. It must have just been emotion."

God requires us, however, to give the same amount of time, effort and energy to chaff as we give to wheat. Unfortunately, we don't know which is which until later in the process.

Two Bible Studies

I teach Bible studies to people in their homes. The studies are basically a synopsis of the entire Bible in 12 weeks. I was teaching one such course to a young professional couple who seemed very keen to learn. A few lessons into it, the man asked me if he could invite one of his colleagues to join us. I said yes.

A single lady joined us for our next lesson. During and after the lesson, I couldn't help but think the woman would not last long. For whatever reason, it didn't appear she had the personality that really wanted to serve God. On the other hand, as far as I could tell, the couple was going to be foundational leaders in the church. Or so I

CHAFF

thought.

The man and his wife, as well as their colleague, all turned to God and were born again. A year or so later, the man and his family began to fade and they finally stopped coming to church altogether. The single woman, however, grew spiritually. Today, she is married, and she and her husband have started a church.

You really never know who is chaff and who is wheat until further into the process. The key is to be faithful to God and be careful not to judge a person based on **your** understanding. You cannot qualify or disqualify a person in living for God. They will do it themselves as they go through the purpose and process in life.

> **You cannot qualify or disqualify a person in living for God.**

In scripture, there seems to be some distinction between three groups of people: the righteous, the ungodly, and the sinners. Once a person is saved, they are no longer in the general group of sinners. After a person turns to God and is born again, there seems to be two classifications of children of God: the righteous and the ungodly.

*And if the righteous scarcely be saved, where shall the ungodly **and** the sinner appear?*
1 Peter 4:18

The ungodly are not so: but are like the chaff which the wind driveth away. Therefore the ungodly shall not

WILL I SURVIVE?

stand in the judgment, nor sinners in the congregation of the righteous. For the LORD knoweth the way of the righteous: but the way of the ungodly shall perish.
Psalm 1:4-6

At some point, we shall all stand before the One True God of the Bible. Sinners will receive judgment because they did not submit to God at all. The ungodly, or those who have not become godly, will also be judged, but from a completely different dimension than the sinner. The ungodly did turn to God, but did not allow the process of sanctification to take place, so that they could be conformed into the image of Christ.

So what do most Christians do with new converts, the sheaves? We tip-toe around them, and make sure we are religiously correct, so not to "offend" them in any way. What does God do with new converts? He puts them on the threshing, winnowing and sifting floor to find out if they are chaff or wheat. Sheaves do not automatically go on to become flour. First, they go to the threshing floor.

Threshing

Threshing is the process of removing the grain of wheat from the stalk and husk. Here the edible part of the wheat is separated from the inedible chaff, which surrounds it. Threshing is completed in a few different ways.

Essential to the threshing process is the threshing floor. It is a flat area of hard dirt or rock on which freshly

CHAFF

harvested wheat is piled. When there is only a little wheat, the kernels of grain can be knocked off of the stalk with a stick or a flail, which is what Gideon was doing when he was trying to hide the fact that he had harvested some wheat (Judges 6:11).

The stick, properly named flail, comes from the Latin word *tribulum*, which is where we get our English word tribulation, or trouble. God threshes a small harvest with trouble. Why is it that the moment something goes wrong, we want to start giving all the credit to the devil? Difficulties are all a part of God's purpose and process. He uses a little tribulation and trouble to separate the chaff from the grain of wheat.

Trust me, I could speak a lot about tribulation and trouble. The applications are innumerable in our daily life. You may not be able to control what happens to you, but you can control what happens within you. Stop kicking every time tribulation or trouble finds you. God is **not** against you. There's just some chaff, which needs to be loosened and broken off. Learn to say, "Yes Lord." Choose to become a better person, not a bitter one.

> I cannot control what happens to me, but I can control what happens within me.

A much more common way of threshing, is to pile the sheaves on the threshing floor, and drive cows or oxen back and forth over it. By walking on the sheaves, their feet "threshed" the grain from the stalk. With the repeated walking, their weight would separate the chaff

WILL I SURVIVE?

from the wheat.

There is a very interesting parallel here, as most of the grain of wheat are threshed or separated from the stock by the heavy weight of the thresher. In this case, the thresher is ministerial leadership, in particular, the Pastor.

Most Pastors will do almost anything not to lose people. God's intent, however, is to find out if a person is chaff or wheat. To that end, Pastors often work against the will and purpose of God.

When I was a Pastor, I would make a statement from the pulpit about every three of four months, which went something like this:

"It's not a matter of 'if,' but 'when' I say something that you may take offence to. It is not my intent to purposely offend anyone, but I am a man of God, and I try to deliver what He is saying to prepare us for Heaven. Therefore, it is only a matter of time before I will say something that will, inadvertently, step on your toes. So when this happens, don't be shocked. Don't be offended. Understand what's happening. Conviction is from God."

When we speak as the oracle of God, we will step on the carnality of man. Those are the times we are somewhat anxious to get back to church for the next service, to see who survived, to find out who is wheat and who is chaff.

This is why some TV ministries are invalid. They seldom preach anything to separate the chaff from the wheat. Who wants to hear some Preacher tell you if you

CHAFF

will send in $100 they guarantee you will have trouble come your way? In our world of political and religious correctness, they do not want to "offend" any offerings that may come in. We cannot make bread out of chaff, and with all of the politically correct preaching it's easy to start to wonder how much of the true body of Christ exists.

It is also interesting to note, in the threshing process God made sure those who did the threshing work were well cared for and kept. The Lord commanded, "Do not muzzle an ox while it is treading out the grain" (Deut. 25:4). In other words, the ox, or preacher, is allowed to benefit materially from his labor by eating all that is needed of the grain he is threshing.

Many farmers own a "threshing sled," a piece of equipment that looks like a wide toboggan with pieces of metal or stone set in the bottom so the wheat could be cut off the stalk faster.

> . . . *I will make you into a new threshing sledge with sharp teeth. . . . thresh the mountains and beat them small, and make the hills like chaff.*
> **Isaiah 41:15**

As the oxen or threshing sled went over and over the large pile of harvested wheat, the stalks would be cut up into pieces. The heads of grain would fall off the stalk and often separate from the husk. The process continued until the farmer, or the husbandman, checked to see that

WILL I SURVIVE?

all the grain of wheat were off the stock. At this point, the grain was ready to be "winnowed."

Winnowing

As the threshing continued by (1) the flail, or trouble, or (2) the ox, the preacher, the grain of wheat sank lower and lower in the pile because there was substance to it. The chaff, because there is no substance to it, floated to the surface.

Are you beginning to see the difference between chaff and wheat within the church? The preacher preaches and delivers a message from the Lord. For one person, the Word of the Lord pricks their heart and they seek an altar. "Oh God, whatever You want; I'm Yours," they pray. For another person, an attitude begins to serge, "Who does he think he is? I have a life. I don't need this."

At this point, the winnowing process begins. There is a separation within the mixed pile of grain, stalk, and husk, so the edible grain can be sifted and eaten. To winnow the grain, the farmer scoops up the pieces of the crop he has just threshed and throws it all up into the air.

To the untrained eye, it would seem all hell had broken loose in the church. Everything goes topsy-turvy! All a Pastor can do is pray because when the winnowing starts, you do not know which way it's going to go.

That we should no longer be children, tossed to and fro and carried about with every wind of doctrine,

CHAFF

by the trickery of men, in the cunning craftiness of deceitful plotting.
Ephesians 4:14

The harvester would throw the chaff and wheat up into the air using a winnowing fork, or shovel; similar to the way people today move loose hay with a pitchfork. The wind would blow the light pieces of chaff stalk to the side, while the grain of wheat, which is heavier, would fall almost straight back down. Over time, the threshing floor would be covered with distinct piles of material: the kernels of grain, which fell almost straight down, and the pieces of chaff or straw, which would be blown further away.

In Biblical lands, grain crops ripened in April, May, and June. During the daytime, there was usually too little wind to winnow. The farmer had to wait until there was a slight wind, which often came in the evening. We see this issue referenced in the book of Ruth, when Naomi told Ruth to go see Boaz in the evening while he was winnowing barley on the threshing floor (Ruth 3:2).

Not once, but twice God said to satan, "Have you considered My servant Job?" God actually gave satan permission to find out if Job was wheat or chaff. God gave permission for satan to take Job to the threshing floor for the threshing, winnowing and sifting process.

Be assured, it is not **if**, but **when** the wind blows, the chaff will be blown away as there is no substance to it. On the other hand, wheat will stay and settle back down

WILL I SURVIVE?

at the feet of the winnower, Jesus.

There is no doubt at all, life's wind is blowing. If it hasn't hit you already, it's coming. If not this month, then next month, but either way it is coming. The question is, are you wheat or chaff? It is your choice so stop pointing and casting blame.

It's not if, but when the winds of adversity blow, the chaff will be blown away.

Without understanding God's purpose and process in life, it can be disheartening when you compare a relatively small pile of wheat to the huge piles of sheaves that came in from the field. At times, I struggle when I see all the people come into the church, and then I sit helpless as I watch them go. And I whisper a prayer, *"Lord, forgive them, for they know not what they are doing."* God is looking for wheat.

The process of winnowing provides a clear picture of how God will treat people on Judgment Day. The people who have believed in Him and have lived obedient lives will be treated as wheat. He will gather them together for safe-keeping.

I sit helplessly watching as people leave. And I whisper a prayer, "Lord, forgive them, for they know not what they are doing."

In contrast, the unbelievers and disobedient will be treated as chaff. They will burn in the lake of fire just as chaff is burned up in an oven. The next chapter will give further revelation on the subject and purpose of *the fire*. The following scripture is a precursor.

CHAFF

His winnowing fan is in His hand, and He will thoroughly clean out His threshing floor, and gather His wheat into the barn; but He will burn up the chaff with unquenchable fire.
Matthew 3:12

Sifting

The process of separating chaff from wheat must be over, isn't it? No, not yet. Just before the wheat grain is ready to be ground into flour, it must be sifted. Sifting is necessary for a number of reasons. It was common during harvesting that small pebbles and weed seeds would mix in with the wheat.

The threshing and winnowing did not always separate the wheat from the extra non-chaff parts. As well, the winnowing process did not remove 100 percent of the chaff from the grain, requiring further purging and separation. You see, God wants every part of you to be holy.

But as the One Who called you is holy, you yourselves also be holy in all your conduct and manner of living.
1 Peter 1:15 AMP

In Biblical culture, a grain sift was round and fairly large, usually two to three feet in diameter. The sides were wooden and often 3-5 inches high, with a bottom often made of woven reeds or grass. The process of sifting was

WILL I SURVIVE?

such a common part of life, often people felt no need to describe it.

Jesus addressed the process of sifting when He referenced to it to Peter:

> *And the Lord said, "Simon, Simon! Indeed, Satan has asked for you, that he may sift you as wheat. But I have prayed for you, that your faith should not fail; and when you have returned to Me, strengthen your brethren."*
> **Luke 22:31-32**

Herein lies spiritual maturity and a sign of true conversion: you begin to realize life is not all about you. Simon Peter, after you get through the process and are conformed into His image, *"strengthen your brethren."* Go beyond yourself and help others through the process in life.

The wheat grains are placed into the sifter and the shaking begins. Wheat stays in the sifter, and everything else is sifted out. The parallel here is the removal of our carnal humanity as we are sanctified and conformed into His image (Romans 8:29; 12:2). Trust me, the sifting and shaking process is no fun. That which can be shaken free, will be shaken free and away from the body of Christ.

> *All your strongholds are fig trees with ripened figs: If they are shaken, They fall into the mouth of the eater.*
> **Nahum 3:12**

CHAFF

Whose voice then shook the earth; but now He has promised, saying, "Yet once more I shake not only the earth, but also heaven." Now this, "Yet once more," indicates the removal of those things that are being shaken, as of things that are made, that the things which cannot be shaken may remain.
Hebrews 12:26-27

After the threshing, winnowing and sifting process, the valuable grain was gathered and moved into storage. I will cover the topic of storage in another chapter. No matter where you may find yourself in the process, one thing is so very vital and crucial: **don't abort the process.** God will never leave nor forsake you (Deuteronomy 13:6). However, we can leave Him by pulling the plug on the process. There will be times when things seem to go slowly and are no doubt difficult, but don't stop. Keep going.

The LORD is with you while you are with Him. If you seek Him, He will be found by you; but if you forsake Him, He will forsake you.
2 Chronicles 15:2

The harvester handled the chaff in a few different ways. Sometimes he used the chaff to make mud bricks. Sometimes he used it as fuel for household ovens, because it burned fast and hot. Most of the time, he ignored the chaff and left it to blow away.

WILL I SURVIVE?

Therefore I will scatter them like stubble that passes away by the wind of the wilderness.
Jeremiah 13:24

In December 2006, a devastating windstorm struck Stanley Park in Vancouver, Canada. With winds exceeding 71 mph, the storm leveled over 100 acres of forest, causing extensive damage with an estimated 10,000 trees downed.

On Vancouver Island, "Big Mother," the fourth largest red cedar in Canada was impacted by the storm. The ancient giant stood over 154 feet tall with a circumference of almost 56 feet. It had withstood many storms for over 1,000 years before it finally toppled in one of life's windstorms.

Will you survive? The winds of adversity will come and it does not matter who or where you are. There is great comfort, however, when you begin to understand God's purpose for the process He uses in your life.

Whatever happens, don't abort the process.

6

THE FIRE

Before going on with the analogy and theme of the bread making process, I need to elaborate and bring further revelation and understanding regarding God's purpose and process in life.

For our God is a consuming fire.
Hebrews 12:29

I remember an older Pastor friend sharing one of his many ministry experiences. He spent many months praying and fasting, seeking God for revival in the church. Over a few short months he went from 123 tithe payers to 62. That's quite a blow to the morale as well as to the church budget.

The Pastor sought the Lord for understanding and insight as to what was happening. I will never forget the answer that came. The Lord spoke to him and acknowledged his prayer request for revival had indeed been answered, therefore, giving him revival! Say what?

We need to settle something here: God is the Almighty One and in charge of **all** things. The devil is

WILL I SURVIVE?

not almighty and can only act according to the will and purpose of God. God sees the heart and intent of man and will use whatever means necessary to prepare His church for His return. These last days are not the time to play around in living for God. It's time to be real and let the Spirit of God mold and shape you into His image.

A Metaphor

I cannot think of a better way to describe the enthusiasm, zeal, excitement and joy of a believer than the phrase *"on fire for the Lord."* How about, *"I feel the fire"* . . . ? The phrases do not mean a person is literally on fire; they are metaphors.

A metaphor is a figure of speech in which a term or phrase is attributed, but not literally applicable, in order to suggest resemblance or comparison. You've heard metaphors before. Here's one: *My right hand man.* It does not mean there is a literal man growing out of my right hand. It is a metaphor expressing the value and importance of a person.

His presence warmed the room. He may look good, but he was not literally as hot as a furnace, where people could warm themselves from his heat!

The goal keeper was a rock. Actually, he was human and played rather well. The team did not place a literal rock in the goal net to keep guard! You get the idea.

A sea of troubles. There are troubles out there, but you will not find a literal sea tossed about with a host of

THE FIRE

troubles.

The Bible uses the word "fire" as metaphor.

When the Day of Pentecost had fully come,
. . . suddenly there came a sound from heaven, as of a rushing mighty wind, and it filled the whole house where they were sitting. Then there appeared to them divided tongues, as of fire, and one sat upon each of them. And they were all filled with the Holy Spirit and began to speak with other tongues, as the Spirit gave them utterance.
Acts 2:1-4

The subject and emphasis here was the fact people received the Holy Ghost and spoke in tongues, not that there was some sort of literal fire sitting on each one. Fire was a descriptive word depicting the appearance of something that looked like a tongue of fire. Speaking in tongues, or in another language, was the sign and evidence of the Holy Spirit's presence. Thus the description in Acts 2:4.

….But his word was in mine heart as a burning fire shut up in my bones, and I was weary with forbearing, and I could not stay.
Jeremiah 20:9

The writers of the Bible used the word fire many times throughout the scriptures. Not only did they use fire to describe the presence of God and the passionate conviction within a believer, it was also is symbolic of destruction, hell, judgment, and wrath. It is used to convey persecution, trials and tribulation, burning, purging, consumption and destruction.

In using fire as a metaphor, writers compare and associate the attributes of fire to a subject. Perhaps it burns like fire, or it looks like fire, or it feels like fire. You get the idea.

With that in mind, pay close attention to the illustration Matthew gives regarding God's purpose and process in life.

And even now the ax is laid to the root of the trees. Therefore every tree which does not bear good fruit is cut down and thrown into the fire.
Matthew 3:10

We are not talking about a light trim or prune here. There is an ax, and the target is the root and foundation of the tree that does not show growth, maturity and fruitfulness. The discourse denotes the tree is to be cut down. You and I are tested and tried by our lives and productivity, not by our birth or profession.

The Fire

I indeed baptize you with water unto repentance, but He who is coming after me is mightier than I, whose

THE FIRE

sandals I am not worthy to carry. He will baptize you with the Holy Spirit and fire.
Matthew 3:11

How many times have you heard someone who has just received the Baptism of the Holy Spirit say, *"I feel the fire"*...? We've got to keep the "fire." Fiery excitement and a sense of celebration comes with the Baptism of the Holy Spirit!

Many think of the scripture in Acts 1:8: *"But you shall receive **power** when the Holy Spirit has come upon you,"* and refer to power as the fire. They say things such as, "We must pray until we have the 'fire of the Holy Ghost' flowing in us."

Fire is a good analogy for describing the Holy Spirit. We do receive "power" and it does feel like "fire shut up in our bones." However, that is not what is meant in the verses mentioned. When we receive the Holy Spirit, we are also baptized with fire. The two go hand in hand. The next verse explains the baptism of fire.

*His winnowing fan is in His hand, and **He** will thoroughly clean out His threshing floor, and gather His wheat into the barn; but **He** will burn up the chaff with unquenchable fire.*
Matthew 3:12

This verse brings clarity, understanding and a sense of the process once someone receives the Holy Spirit of

WILL I SURVIVE?

God. In light of the message of my entire book, let me give you context before explaining further.

Understand God wills, desires and wants you to enter Heaven. There's just one little detail you must remember, some things are **not** permitted there.

> *But there shall by no means enter in anything that defiles, or causes an abomination or a lie…*
> **Revelation 21:27**

> *But as He who called you is holy, you also be holy in all your conduct, because it is written, "Be holy, for I am holy."*
> **1 Peter 1:15-16**

God is Holy and holiness is a requirement to go to Heaven. Hebrews 12:14 says, "…***holiness***, *without which no man shall see the Lord."* Do not confuse righteousness with holiness. We have the righteousness of the Lord, based on His sacrifice on the cross. Righteousness is what He gives us. Holiness is what we give to Him based on our relationship with Him. We are instructed and required to be holy in all manner of conduct. The greater meaning here is that we are to be holy in all areas of behavior and character.

When you read the Bible for all its worth, you will find scriptures filled with instruction for us in our walk and relationship with the Almighty One True God. It is indeed life impacting. That is, scripture is intended to change our entire being; our very nature is to be transformed.

How does that compare to today's mindset that our "Christian duty" consists of our obligated one hour Sunday morning church service? And maybe, if you feel like it, a mid-week Bible study.

> *Humble yourselves under the mighty hand of God…*
> **1 Peter 5:6**

> *Be sober, be vigilant; because your adversary the devil walks about like a roaring lion, seeking whom he may devour. Resist him, steadfast in the faith, knowing that the same sufferings are experienced by your brotherhood in the world. But may the God of all grace, who called us to His eternal glory by Christ Jesus, after you have suffered a while, perfect, establish, strengthen, and settle you.*
> **1 Peter 5:8-10**

Did you just read the scripture correctly? The God of all grace gives you over to *suffering for a while*? You mean we are supposed to go through and experience some difficulties which in turn, will help establish and make us strong? Correct. These sufferings are to perfect, or complete us.

We can suffer and be

> **Our righteousness or standing, is based on Jesus' sacrifice for us. Holiness, or right living, is what we do for Him, based on our relationship with Him.**

established, or we can be like the religious masses described in the following scripture:

These people draw near to Me with their mouth, And honor Me with their lips, But their heart is far from Me. And in vain they worship Me, Teaching as doctrines the commandments of men. When He had called the multitude to Himself, He said to them, Hear and understand
Matthew 15:8-10

These verses never cease to astound me. There are good people who truly and honestly worship Jesus, but the Bible says it is vain worship; it's going nowhere. Why? It's vain because in reality it's lip service without practical and tangible expression. It is simply the result of individuals who are practicing a religious tradition, based on man's beliefs, doctrines and commandments.

God is Spirit, and those who worship Him must worship in spirit and truth. **John 4:24**

Perhaps the requirement to worship was part of the reasoning behind the Apostle Paul's instruction to *"work out your own salvation with fear and trembling."* I strongly encourage you to adopt the philosophy of asking for chapter and verse when someone gives you a supposed scriptural answer to your spiritual questions.

You and I must be ready to always obey the Word of

THE FIRE

God. We are responsible for searching the scriptures and knowing them for ourselves, and not simply putting our trust in people, no matter how nice or well-meaning they may be (Philippians 2:12; 2 Timothy 3:16).

Of course, when a spiritual leader makes absolute statements that actually require people to **do** things as a result of their belief in God, some will become offended, which is what happened in Matthew 15. The disciples came up to Jesus and told Him the religious people of the day were offended by His comments.

Okay, I need to say it again. If your Pastor or Spiritual leadership are true men and women of God, and speak as the mouthpiece of God, then it's not *if* but **when** you will be offended and take exception to something they say.

Now, in understanding some of God's purpose and plan, how will you respond the next time you begin to feel offended? Your response will determine how far you go in the bread-making process, being formed into His image.

> *Then said he unto the disciples, It is impossible but that offences will come…*
> **Luke 17:1**

Jesus flat out says it is a part of life; **offences will come!** Oh, no one offended you this week? Well, next week is just around the corner! You had a good month? No worries, another month is coming! Trust me, offences will come.

WILL I SURVIVE?

Purge or Purify

In Matthew 3:11 John the Baptist said, God will baptize you with the Holy Ghost, and at the same time He will baptize you with fire. So what is the fire? Verse 12 enlightens us as to what happens in the baptism of fire. For the sake of remembrance, I'll quote it again.

> *His winnowing fan is in His hand, and He will thoroughly clean out His threshing floor, and gather His wheat into the barn; but He will burn up the chaff with unquenchable fire.*
> **Matthew 3:12**

Notice the prop referred to in this verse is a fan. And the fan is in whose hand? It's in God's hand. In relation to fire, a fan is used as an instrument to blow or ignite the fire, to make it burn hotter. Here, God brings unquenchable fire into the threshing, winnowing and sifting process. The purpose is to burn up all the chaff, and anything that is not wheat.

God allows and sends fire into our lives to do one of two things: it will purify, or it will purge. Adversity or offences in life will purify the old, carnal fallen nature out of you, in preparation for Heaven. Or, it will purge you out of the Body, the church of the living God. If in the process you begin to have an attitude and chip on your shoulder, or become offended and do not forgive, you will thereby disqualify yourself from Heaven's door.

THE FIRE

All believers will be baptized with fire. Do you have a problem with anger? God will allow and even send many opportunities for you to deal with your anger. Your buttons will be pushed! Have a problem with sexual sin? Along will come an opportunity to view sexually illicit pictures, or a person who also struggles with sexual sin will make themselves available. What if you struggle with dishonesty? You get the idea. Out of nowhere, will appear an opportunity for you to choose honesty or dishonesty.

**The fire will purify, or it will purge.
All believers will be baptized with fire.**

Is God tempting you? **No**, He is not, but He is baptizing you with fire. He's giving you an opportunity to allow the carnal sin areas to be purified and purged out of you. Do you understand the idea? Everyone is salted with fire.

For everyone will be seasoned with fire, and every sacrifice will be seasoned with salt. Salt is good, but if the salt loses its flavor, how will you season it? Have salt in yourselves, and have peace with one another.
Mark 9:49-50

The phrase *"the salt loses its flavor"* means the salt has lost its usefulness, or is lacking savor. Some people are void of qualities that define a godly spirit and character. You call yourself a Christian, but you're not really Christ-

WILL I SURVIVE?

like.

Salt, in this verse, also means prudence, or good judgment and discretion. People who lack saltiness do not have preserving properties concerning the practical affairs of life. They do not understand God's purpose and process.

Paraphrased, some people become bent out of shape, displaying an attitude when something happens to them. They do not allow the situation or circumstance to purify them. They are too easily offended and therefore their lives are not productive for God's kingdom.

Looking carefully lest anyone fall short of the grace of God; lest any root of bitterness springing up cause trouble, and by this many become defiled . . .
Hebrews 12:15

Offences **will** come, and if not dealt with, offenses **will** defile many people. Here, the word "defile" means to contaminate or taint. To the enemy of your soul, it does not matter at all if you miss Heaven by an inch or a mile, by a murderous evil act or by an impure thought. Either way, you're toast.

However, if you understand what's happening through the purpose and the process of life, you can choose to become better and not bitter using the situation and circumstance as a stepping stone, not a stumbling block. You can allow the fan to purify your spirit and mind and grow in grace and in the knowledge of our Lord Jesus

THE FIRE

To the enemy of your soul, it does not matter at all if you miss Heaven by an inch or a mile.

(2 Peter 3:18).

What we must be very careful not to do is abort the process. The promise of salvation is only to those who "endure to the end" (Matthew 10:22). That means you and I stay under God's fan and allow it to do what it is intended to do: purify us and conform us into His image.

For the time will come when they will not endure sound doctrine; but after their own lusts shall they heap to themselves teachers, having itching ears; And they shall turn away their ears from the truth, and shall be turned unto fables.
2 Timothy 4:3-4

God always gives us a choice. Matter-a-fact, I would go so far as to say, that if there is no choice, it is not God. In all of life's matters, we have a choice. Will the offence, situation, or circumstance purify me from sin, or purge me out of the church? We always have a choice.

Jesus had to take drastic measures when He was trying to save Saul of Tarsus. He interjected into his life with a statement, *"it is hard for thee to kick against the pricks"* (Acts 9:4-6 KJV). Paraphrased, he said, "Stop fighting Me. I'm at work here trying to save you."

Remember the Old Testament story of Joseph and all of the bad, awful, terrible things that happened to him?

WILL I SURVIVE?

Joseph finally learned to accept the process. By forgiving his brothers, he developed godly character. So much so, that he later said, *"So now it was not you that sent me hither, but God. But as for you, ye thought evil against me; but God meant it unto good"* (Genesis 50:20 KJV).

God always gives us a choice.

God is on His throne, and all is well. He is the only wise God and Savior, totally and completely sovereign. I choose to humble myself to His rule and authority here on earth. I know there is an adversary and enemy of my soul. He is not in control, nor is he all-powerful. This old world is not my home and I am more than willing to let go of anything and all things that cause me to hold on to it. I desire to be conformed into His image and likeness, by His grace.

John the Baptist gave us a forewarning about receiving the Spirit of God. We will be introduced to the fire of tribulation as we move onto the threshing floor. It is in this life now that we determine what will happen in the next life. Our response to life here will reveal if we are wheat or chaff. Our judgment is not subjective, as in the Old Testament when people did what was right in their own eyes. Our judgment will be objective, based on God's Word, which will judge all in the last day (Revelation 20).

It is in this life now, that we determine what will happen in the next life.

No one is exempt or given a

THE FIRE

pass out of God's purpose and process. What's amazing is what happened in the very next chapter of Matthew. Remember Jesus was God manifested in the flesh, Holy God and fully man. Just after John's enlightened revelation of being baptized with the Holy Ghost and with fire, we read:

Then Jesus was led up by the Spirit into the wilderness to be tempted by the devil.
Matthew 4:1

Jesus is led, brought and directed by the Spirit of God, for the sole and primary purpose of being tempted by the devil! Hello, is this for real? It can't be the will of God to be tempted and go through hard times! Oh, wait a minute… I guess it does say the Spirit led him to be tempted, doesn't it?

Though He was a Son, yet He learned obedience by the things which He suffered. And having been perfected, He became the author of eternal salvation to all who obey Him. ***Hebrews 5:8-9***

What is the purpose of the fire again? What is it supposed to do exactly?

That He might sanctify and cleanse her with the washing of water by the word, that He might present her to Himself a glorious church, not having spot or

WILL I SURVIVE?

wrinkle or any such thing, but that she should be holy and without blemish.
Ephesians 5:26-27

Wrinkles

Have you ever washed your clothes? Of course you have. I just laundered mine yesterday. Laundry is not difficult in today's world. You simply sort the colors and put them into a washing machine. Less than an hour later, you take them out and put them in the dryer. Usually less than an hour later the clothes are dry; you take them out of the dryer, fresh and clean.

Aside from the washing, if you leave your clothes sitting in the dryer for any length of time, you have another little problem: wrinkles. I wear a lot of dress shirts and I want them to look good. How do you remove wrinkles? Apply, with pressure and perhaps steam, one very hot iron and voila!

Do you have wrinkles in your life, or in your character? Don't mind God's hot iron pressing down. You won't break. If you allow the process to continue, you will be a better person for it.

Each one's work will become clear; for the Day will declare it, because it will be revealed by fire; and the fire will test each one's work, of what sort it is.
1 Corinthians 3:13

THE FIRE

As the baptism of fire comes to purify or purge, and as God irons out a few wrinkles and impurities in your life, *"things"* will begin to come to the surface of your conscious mind. There may be slight attitudes and flaws, or perhaps bigger issues, which have been buried for years. You do not have to relive the past, but you do need to forgive it, and allow the impurities to be sifted out of your life.

My Exercise Program

Life happens to the best of us. I'm sure we all have felt like singing the song, *"Nobody knows the trouble I've seen. Nobody knows my sorrow."* If you and I were to take the time to sit down over coffee and be real and honest, I'm sure you could tell me some stories that may surprise me as to what's happened in your life. I too could probably cause you to shake your head in disbelief and amazement if I were to share my stories.

I don't exactly remember when I consciously began to think about life and all that happens as a part of God's purpose and process. I previously had a lot of thoughts on the subject, and understood the basic principles, but the big picture wasn't clearly defined. I suppose clarity started as I was lying in bed with a broken leg, after being betrayed and abandoned by family and friends.

The Lord began to speak to me about a number of things. Starting an exercise program was His top priority. Now, I'm on a stringent exercise program. I exercise every

WILL I SURVIVE?

single day, and some days, multiple times. The program is called Acts 24:16:

**And herein do I exercise myself,
to have always a conscience void of offence
toward God, and toward men.
Acts 24:16 KJV**

In this verse, to exercise means to take great pains over, by training or discipline. The root word gives the idea of putting a sword in a sheaf. That is, stop fighting and quit opposing what God is doing.

The Bible instructs us not to judge anything before its time. I like how the New Living Translation puts this verse.

So don't make judgments about anyone ahead of time—before the Lord returns. For he will bring our darkest secrets to light and will reveal our private motives. Then God will give to each one whatever praise is due.
1 Corinthians 4:5 NLT

I remember a time when I was somewhat annoyed about a situation. I was left brooding and generally not overly happy. As I was talking to the Lord about it, well more like off-loading my thoughts, the Lord spoke: *"Celebrate My sovereignty."* His words stopped me dead in my tracks. Sovereignty? God is in complete and total

THE FIRE

control.

What a novel idea! I smiled, and half chuckled. Then I shook my head in revelation. After asking the Lord's forgiveness, I began to thank and actually worship Jesus each time I was reminded of the situation. His purpose will manifest in spite of my objections. I might as well worship Him through it. God is on His throne, and all is well.

Offence

An offence is something which leads to error or sin. It is the trap to which the bait is attached, hence the trap itself. To make Heaven my home, I must be void of offence. That means I should not take offence, and equally should not be offensive.

Whatever happens, I purpose not to go astray and off track from my walk and relationship with God. I understand the purpose and process. I'm not taking the bait, which would only leave me trapped in this bad, awful situation.

Remember Jesus' comments in Luke 17, when he said *offences will come*? Well, in Matthew's account of the same story, Peter asks the question, "How many times do I put up with this jerk? Seven times?" (I just slightly paraphrased his question.) Jesus responded, "Actually, you need to forgive seventy times seven." That equals 490 times per day. Allowing for a little sleep time, that's approximately once every 2.83 seconds.

WILL I SURVIVE?

While going through one of the lowest times of my life, a time when my church leaders betrayed me unmercifully in judgment, the Lord brought the Luke 17 story to my mind. Then He asked me, *"Who hates you so much, that they would offend you every 2.83 seconds?"* I gave some serious and honest consideration to the question before replying, "No one Lord. I don't know of anyone who hates me that much."

All of a sudden, it was as if a hidden trap door opened and I realized there must be a deeper, greater meaning to the story. Revelation flooded my soul. It's not that someone hates me and offends me every 2.83 seconds. It's that I get offend once, and when I do not forgive and release it I think of that hurt about every 2.83 seconds and re-offend myself.

Peter received the revelation. Forgiveness is one of those "God" qualities and characteristics that comes and grows in you, by going through the process. It is the result of allowing Christ to be formed in you. Forgiveness makes room for the new man to step forward and allows the old man to fade away.

I was stunned by the revelation. The Lord began to draw me back to the request of the disciples, found in Luke 17. The disciples witnessed first-hand Jesus' many mighty miracles and wonders, yet this is the only time they requested: *"Lord, increase our faith"* (Luke 17:5). The whole forgiveness thing is a big deal. Matter-a-fact, it's a deal breaker.

THE FIRE

Pursue peace with all people, and holiness, without which no one will see the Lord: looking carefully lest anyone fall short of the grace of God; lest any root of bitterness springing up cause trouble, and by this many become defiled...
Hebrews 12:14-15

Unforgiveness is where bitterness grows. Bitterness is the acid that destroys the container; and that container that is destroyed is you. When you are bitter, you become defiled, tainted and contaminated. You disqualify yourself and abort the process.

Many books have been written on the subject of forgiveness. The revelation of forgiveness is that forgiveness is not about the other person, how wrong they were and how right you are. Forgiveness is about you. If you don't forgive and let go of the offence not only will the Lord **not** forgive you, but hurt will grow in you and eventually disqualify you from God's purpose and process for your life.

Last summer I was preaching in the Toronto area, and, as is my custom, I went for a walk. I was not thinking of anything in particular, just walking in fellowship with the Lord. All of a sudden, words came out of my mouth, and I heard myself forgiving and releasing forgiveness toward those

> **Unforgiveness is where bitterness grows. Bitterness is the acid that destroys the container; and that container that is destroyed, is you.**

WILL I SURVIVE?

who violated, judged and hurt me.

I had already forgiven them, repeatedly and constantly. Every time my memory would bring it up, I would forgive and release forgiveness. But this time was different. I remember hearing these words rise out of my spirit and come out of my mouth:

"Lord Jesus, not only do I forgive them, but I am asking that You not hold this against them in judgment. Wipe it from their account. Do not hold it against them. Make it as if it never happened on their account.

"In fact, I am asking You not to call upon me to testify against them. When we all stand in judgment I do not want to give testimony against them.

"I am asking Jesus, that you bless them. They really do not know what they are doing. And I am asking that You be merciful and kind to them. I want them to be saved. Let Your Spirit touch their hearts and lives. Bless them, Jesus. Bless them."

I was completely stunned. It happened so fast. As I kept walking, a smile came on my face and I remember saying, *"Wow, Jesus. You are at work in me. Maybe I am growing spiritually through all this."*

What I did not know until three months later was at the exact time the words were coming out of my spirit, the people I was forgiving were making decisions of judgment and abandonment against me. God knows all things. What's of the utmost importance is that I keep a good spirit and attitude. I have one goal in life: to have a personal intimate relationship with Jesus. I want to be like

THE FIRE

Him. And I want to make Heaven my home. Whatever I need to do to accomplish this mission will be well worth it. Eternity is too long to miss.

Most every Christian knows the Lord's Prayer. It was one of the first things we memorized growing up, or attending church. All the essentials are in that little prayer. It comes right out and says our Heavenly Father will not forgive us if we do not first forgive others.

> *Our Father which art in heaven, Hallowed be thy name. Thy kingdom come. Thy will be done in earth, as it is in heaven. Give us this day our daily bread. And forgive us our debts, as we forgive our debtors. And lead us not into temptation, but deliver us from evil: For thine is the kingdom, and the power, and the glory, forever. Amen. For if ye forgive men their trespasses, your heavenly Father will also forgive you: But if ye forgive not men their trespasses, neither will your Father forgive your trespasses.*
> **Matthew 6:9-15 KJV**

Later on in Chapter 18 of the book of Matthew, Jesus further illustrates the truth of the forgiveness principle by saying that if a person does not forgive, he will be delivered over to the tormentors. Ouch. No one and no circumstance is worth you being tormented, no matter what they've done.

Eternity is too long to miss.

I remember where I was standing, when I had the

WILL I SURVIVE?

conversation with a preacher friend of mine. It was during a time when I was working my way past the memory of hurt and pain. I told him I had expressed my forgiveness toward God for what happened. My friend laughed and laughed. He could not get past the picture of me, a mortal man, forgiving Almighty God.

After he stopped laughing and calmed himself down, I related to him my revelation and view of forgiveness. God is God. My hurt and pain was not about Him; it was about me. God was not hurting; I was. Forgiveness is not about the other person; it is about you.

An offence can come in three areas. You can be offended against God, against others, or against self. For **my** healing and wholeness, I needed to forgive God, others and myself.

I needed to forgive God because from my perspective I really didn't think He showed up when He should have. I began to realize it really bothered me to the point I was offended, even if it was somewhat subconscious.

Obviously, I also had to forgive the perpetrators—the people who hurt me. Again, I needed to forgive for my spiritual wellbeing. It wasn't because they were justified in what they did. I had to forgive for my own eternity's sake.

The last one was the most difficult. It took time for God to reveal to me. I needed to forgive myself. I needed to forgive myself for permitting my circumstance to happen to me. Maybe I could of done something different. No, I couldn't control what happened, or what other people did to me, but I could control how it affected me, and my response to it all. I allowed the pain, hurt and bitterness to stay as long as it did and thus hinder my relationship and walk with Jesus.

I cannot control what happened to me, but I can control how it affects me, and my response to it all.

My Conscience

My exercise program tells me I must always have a conscience void of offence. Here I had another whole new level of revelation come.

The word conscience means co-perception or moral consciousness. It is where we get our sense of right and wrong, and urge to do right. Note the word co-perception has as the prefix "co," which means together, or with perception. It is the act of perceiving or the ability to perceive. Some call it intuition or intuitiveness.

When I allow an unresolved offense to pollute my conscience, my conscience is wounded. The wound is the loss of my "co-," or my partner in perception. For a believer, the "co-" is the voice of the Spirit of the Lord.

As a result of the Spirit of the Lord being removed or silenced, all of my perceptions, my feelings and opinions etc., become the product of human reasoning and judgment. As such, they are unbalanced and unreliable due to the lack of divine input and inspiration. A wounded conscience leaves us with a disposition bent to a fallen nature. That is why some people who isolate themselves can come up with genuinely and sincerely stupid ideas!

Please understand, if you have a wounded conscience, you cannot trust your decisions. They will only produce problems, divisions, disappointments and frustrations. All of this happens because **you** won't forgive and let go.

Forgiveness is all about you. It sets you free to allow your partner, your "co-," the Spirit of God, to flow in and through you! The flow of the Spirit is so powerful and good. With His presence comes His peace, the peace that surpasses, or is superior to all understanding (Philippians 4:7).

It is my sincere prayer that you will not fight the fire. As clay in the Master's hand, allow God to mold and shape you into His image. Step up to the destiny and calling God has for you and let go of unforgiveness, which will only pull you down and make you miserable. Be the better you, not the bitter you. Life can be hard all by itself; you do not need to make it worse by fighting the process.

7
STORAGE

The seed has been sown; the harvest brought in. You survived the threshing, winnowing and sifting process. The fire brought out purity of spirit and character. You are a better and stronger person for allowing the purpose and process of God to continue in your life. You should be good to go. Shouldn't you?

Wheat Is Not Bread

You have progressed and matured in the process. Now you are wheat; however, wheat is not bread. So what do we do with wheat in the bread-making process?

Well, wheat must be placed and stored somewhere for future short-term and long-term use. Some wheat is stored in containers for immediate use over the next few days or weeks. The majority, however, is stored away for winter-time and future use.

We really do like it when God moves quickly. As believers, we often expect it. We work through the process, keeping a good attitude and guarding our spirit. We have waited, and are very willing for change to take

WILL I SURVIVE?

place. Any day now and the supernatural intervention of God will manifest in our lives. When God turns things around for us in a brief period of time, the wheat was stored for short-term use.

I remember talking to a young preacher friend on the phone one day. He was really going through a rough time. There were problems in the church; he was frustrated and filled with anxiety. I asked him how long his trouble had been going on. "Oh, it must be about two weeks now," was his reply.

I was silent for a good 15 or 20 seconds. I didn't know what to say. I tried not to laugh out loud. Was he for real? I couldn't help but think to myself, "Brother, if you can't survive two weeks, you will never survive ministry!" I would wish my troubled waters lasted only two weeks; that would be a picnic, a walk in the park!

**If you faint in the day of adversity,
Your strength is small. Proverbs 24:10**

Reminder to Self

Some wheat is used relatively quickly. It's nice to be part of the short term wheat stash. But for those of us in the long-term storage room, doesn't it just do something to you when you see someone go in and out of life's storms quickly? I mean, where is the fairness?

STORAGE

"For My thoughts are not your thoughts, Nor are your ways My ways," says the LORD. For as the heavens are higher than the earth, So are My ways higher than your ways, And My thoughts than your thoughts.
Isaiah 55:8-9

Without understanding, it's easy to become embittered as God seemingly plays favorites, "blessing" others. Why does God use some wheat quickly, while you are still in the process, waiting?

The message of 2 Corinthians 10:12 tells us it is not wise to compare ourselves among ourselves. You are not all knowing, nor aware of what has, or is transpiring in another person's life. It is best to work out your own salvation (Philippians 2:12) and keep your eyes on Jesus. Let God be God.

It only takes a moment in time for a crisis or wound to occur. It's surviving the healing process that seems to take forever. Healing and wholeness comes only as you continue in the process and move forward towards godliness, even if it's one step at a time. It's easy to quit, drift into obscurity, or settle deep into depression. There is no magic formula or pill. Living takes energy and fortitude, one day at a time.

Sometimes the best thing that you can do is to not think.

Sometimes the best thing you can do is to not think, not ponder, not imagine and not obsess. Just breathe and have faith in God that everything will work out for the best. It's easier to settle into the comfort of the broad way in life, then to do the will of God.

> *Enter by the narrow gate; for wide is the gate and broad is the way that leads to destruction, and there are many who go in by it. Because narrow is the gate and difficult is the way which leads to life, and there are few who find it.*
> **Matthew 7:13-14**

Choose Life

During a time when I felt lost in a dark desert, the Lord impressed me with a thought about the Tree of Life. Remember the story in the Garden of Eden, back in the book of Genesis? God put two trees in the midst of the garden and instructed Adam and Eve not to eat the fruit from these trees.

Why would God even put the trees there if He didn't want people to eat the fruit? Was it a trick? No. You must understand that God, in His wisdom, gave mankind the ultimate power of choice.

Your will to choose is the most powerful possession you have. Nowhere in scripture will you ever find God taking over man's power of choice. God put trees in the midst of the garden to give Adam and Eve, thus mankind, the freedom and ability to choose. You always have a choice.

I choose life. I choose not to surrender or give away

my will to someone or something. Each moment I walked through the dark places of my life, I would think or say out loud, "I choose life." I had no idea what the future held, or how I was going to get through the day. I still chose to live and not to die. Songs such as, "One Day at a Time," by Marijohn Wilking and Kris Kristofferson, came to my mind often during those days. Really, it's the only way we can live: one day at a time.

> "One day at a time sweet Jesus
> That's all I'm askin' of you
> Just give me the strength
> To do every day what I have to do
> Yesterday's gone sweet Jesus
> And tomorrow may never be mine
> Lord, help me today, show me the way
> One day at a time."

Just making the decision to choose life and look to Jesus everyday was such a source of strength and encouragement. The concept of choosing life made such an impact on me. At my brother's woodworking shop, I scrolled out what looks to me like the Tree of Life. I hung it on a wall at my house as a constant reminder to myself to choose life.

WILL I SURVIVE?

Get Out

About 12 or 15 years ago, I took up walking. I use to live in an area where there were paths and hills a person could almost get lost in. So I'd walk, and walk. There is something very therapeutic that comes from getting out of the house or office and into the fresh air, plus it's good for you!

Want to feel better, have more energy and perhaps even live longer? We're talking about surviving life situations, and believe it or not, physical exercise helps. Physical activity stimulates and releases various brain chemicals including endorphins, which create feelings of happiness and euphoria. Studies show exercise can even alleviate symptoms of clinical depression.

A little exercise helps control weight and combats health conditions and diseases. Do you have problems with high blood pressure, cholesterol, diabetes, or concerns about heart disease? Get outside. Just a little exercise can boost your confidence, give you more energy and will even promote better sleep. Physical activity can also help you socially, and give you energy to connect with family or friends.

It would be unbalanced, short sighted and very limiting to focus on only one aspect of your life.

I thought this book was on surviving life situations and understanding God's purpose and process in life? Correct; however, each aspect of our life leads to and is connected to the

STORAGE

others. We are fearfully and wonderfully made, complex in every aspect of our being. You are a combination of spirit, mind, emotions and body. It would be unbalanced, short sighted and very limiting to focus on only one aspect of your life.

If you want to do better emotionally and spiritually, then you also need to do better physically and mentally. What good is it, if you are strong spiritually and weak emotionally, or mentally? It might look good to have a great body, but if you are not spiritually strong you will not endure the process in life.

I take life one day at a time. This year I will walk well over 1,000 kilometers, or just over 620 miles. I did not have a goal, nor did I intend to walk 1,000 kilometers in a year. I just went for a walk as often as I could. Walking is my time. I pray, think, dream, meditate and even try to sing every now and then. I always return energized in my body, mind, spirit and soul. All I did was get out and go for a walk, one kilometer at a time. If you do just a little something every day, it will amaze you where it will lead.

But seek first the kingdom of God and His righteousness, and all these things shall be added to you. Therefore do not worry about tomorrow, for tomorrow will worry about its own things. Sufficient for the day is its own trouble.
Matthew 6:33-34

WILL I SURVIVE?

Pharaoh's Tomb

Most harvested wheat was put into long-term storage for the owner's future use. Many years ago, wheat was stored in jars, sealed and buried in the ground, left alone until needed. Have you ever felt buried and completely alone in the dark?

A good number of years ago, a story hit the news that Archaeologists in Egypt had dug up sealed jars of stored wheat in one of the Pharaoh's tombs. They estimated the wheat was probably 3,000 to 4,000 years old.

One day, scientists examined the grains and decided to do an experiment. They had nothing to lose, so they planted and cared for some of the grains of wheat. Much to their shock and amazement, the wheat grew! After all those years, there was still life in the wheat. It was still alive, though placed in storage, lying dormant for all those years in utter darkness!

I can say, been there, done that, and got the lonely memories to prove it! Weeks turned into months and months into years. How I made it through a day, let alone a week or a month, I'm not always sure. I just kept on walking.

A friend shared with me about another pastor who had been through the ringer. I contacted the minister and invited him to come preach for me. As I was driving him around the beautiful city where I pastored, he looked over to me and said the Lord had spoken a Word for him to give to me.

STORAGE

I gave him permission and invited him to share the Word of the Lord. I was not prepared for what came next. Paraphrased, he told me the city where I pastored was going to be my Gethsemane, the place where I would die. Not die physically, mind you, but the place where I would face myself, my humanity, and all my weaknesses and fears. It would be my testing and pruning ground. What he didn't say was that in order to die, there was going to be some pain.

Quickly dying to self is much preferred; however, when it comes to God's purpose and mankind's nature, often dying out to self takes time. Time seemingly drags on, unmercifully, when you are in the middle of the process.

In order to die, there is going to be some pain.

The Stage of Life

Do you remember what you ate last Tuesday? How about four months ago, on the first Friday? No? Neither do I, but I ate something that nourished and sustained me.

I don't remember how I made it through the vast desert of time during those dark days I went through. I just know I remained in the process and faithful to God, for months and years of waiting, just living for God and doing what I knew to be right.

The Bible is full of great stories that are interesting and even exciting to read. I enjoy preaching from these stories. Then it dawned on me: we only see a very small

WILL I SURVIVE?

portion of each Bible character's entire life. Years upon years took place, of which we have no idea exactly what was going on. We don't know what they had to face, or what they were going through.

As God needed, He pulled each person out of storage and placed him or her on life's stage. Thus their story as we know it begins. As their story unfolded, they did not really understand their purpose in the big scheme of things—not the way you and I know from hindsight. They worked out their salvation trying to allow God to have His way in and through them one day at a time.

Chess

We are a fast paced, instant-microwave society. If we have to wait a whole two seconds for a computer to function, it can be very annoying! Faster and quicker please.

Someone asked me to explain how to be used by God, how to move in the gifts of the Spirit and experience miracles, signs and wonders. I asked if he played chess. "A little; I'm not really good at it," he replied.

I explained each piece could move forward, sideways, or even backwards, depending on the function of the particular piece. Then I asked, "Have you ever seen a chess piece move by itself?" He laughed and replied in the negative.

Then came the revelation: a chess piece cannot move on its own. It simply sits and waits. It is there and available for the Master's hand to direct and move as He sees fit.

STORAGE

Or do you not know that your body is the temple of the Holy Spirit who is in you, whom you have from God, and you are not your own? For you were bought at a price; therefore glorify God in your body and in your spirit, which are God's.
1 Corinthians 6:18-20

You see, our responsibility is to have such a personal and intimate relationship with our Lord Jesus that we trust Him in and for all things. His promise to you is He will never leave or forsake you (Hebrews 13:5). Your worst day in church is still far better than the best day in hell.

The Weakness of God

Because the foolishness of God is wiser than men, and the weakness of God is stronger than men.
1 Corinthians 1:25

When it is time for the wheat to be used, you take the grain of wheat... Wait! How do you make bread from a single grain of wheat? No single individual **is** the body of Christ. The body is made up of many. If you separate yourself from the rest of the body, you will never be what God wants you to be. When you separate yourself, you have no hope

Your worst day in church is still far better than the best day in hell.

of being bread. It's impossible to make bread out of a single grain of wheat.

But now God has set the members, each one of them, in the body just as He pleased. And if they were all one member, where would the body be? But now indeed there are many members, yet one body.
1 Corinthians 12:18-20

For I say, through the grace given to me, to everyone who is among you, not to think of himself more highly than he ought to think, but to think soberly, as God has dealt to each one a measure of faith. For as we have many members in one body, but all the members do not have the same function, so we, being many, are one body in Christ, and individually members of one another.
Romans 12:3-6

Let's be really honest here. Speaking about the body of Christ, there is no such thing as a perfect church. If there were, you and I had better not step in, or it would certainly not remain perfect! We are dealing with fallen human nature, and everyone has one. No one can help rub off the rough edges of your character and spirit like another Brother or Sister. Don't kick against the pricks. You are in a process and it is part of God's purpose.

STORAGE

There comes a greater testimony going through the storms of life then by being snatched out of them.

Held by the Sovereignty of God

Sometimes we get ourselves into a mess, but God will still use our mess for His glory if we work with Him. Too often our attitude will be set on escape. We quickly cry for the Lord to deliver us from where we are and take us out of the trial. Please! Beam me up Scotty!

You want to be delivered, but God wants you to discover. Often, you are trying to escape when God wants you to experience. If He will not take you out, then He'll take you through. **God is looking for some dedicated diligence.** There comes a greater testimony going through the storms of life then by being snatched out of them.

There is a certain tropical bird, which must remain in a cloth-covered cage in order to train it to sing. The bird sits in total darkness, alone. It is the darkness that gives birth to the song. God has a purpose for the darkness. And your destiny is dependent on what you learn when you are covered in darkness.

The LORD will perfect that which concerns me…
Psalm 138:8

WILL I SURVIVE?

Our new-age, modern, and politically correct society is described as smooth, cunning, and plausible; however, it is corrupt in principle and wicked in conduct. All of that must go in order for God's purpose to come to pass.

It is not what happens to us that causes us to grow, but how we respond to what happens to us that causes the growth.

God Did Not Bury You

God did not bury you; He planted you. You are not supposed to shrivel up and die. You are planted to grow. You are in a new place now. Old things are passing away, and all things are becoming new. It's just that the becoming part takes time.

I wish I could hurry things up. So many times I prayed I could fast forward my life. I know all too well the long, lonely nights and endless, slow-moving days. Remember, He didn't bring you this far to leave you.

A grain of wheat has the potential to grow and live; however, the potential is only realized when it is planted. And a planting, if you are not clear on the purpose, feels like a burial.

But He knows the way that I take; when He has tested me, I shall come forth as gold.
Job 23:10
                      It is in stillness that hearing comes.

STORAGE

Be Still

Just last week I was faced with a very difficult and awkward situation. I received news that rocked my world with long rippling effects. My mind was swirling, my heart ached, and my spirit grieved. I did not want to be reactionary. Far too often we "react" rather than "act."

In reacting, you allow the other person or the situation to govern your thoughts and actions. It is so very easy to let others lead you around and play you, like a poor violin. On the other hand, to act is based on your choices and your will. It stems from your character and value system.

In my very volatile situation, the Lord drew my attention to the very familiar Psalm 23: *"The LORD is my shepherd; I shall not want. He makes me to lie down in green pastures; He leads me beside the still waters. He restores my soul…"*

There would most likely be negative consequences if I simply reacted. So for me to act, I need to pause and reflect in order to gain clarity, regarding the entire matter. I wanted and needed to act, and not react, to the situation. I needed to be still before GOD. The word still, gives the idea of rest, sleep or tranquility, to be concealed away from the trouble. You can't think clearly when your emotions and thinking are skewed.

Be still, and know that I am God. Psalm 46:10

WILL I SURVIVE?

You do not struggle or force yourself to be still. Being still is a letting go, a relaxing and a ceasing to strive. It is in stillness that hearing comes. Becoming still is not doing something; it is being in touch with the Lord Jesus from within.

To be still is to experience Jesus in the moment. He is the "I AM." To worship God in the moment, you must live in the now, not mourning the past or worrying about the future. In the stillness, you seek His presence.

If you are going to act with integrity and clarity before God, you must still the beast within.

"I believe in the Sun,
even when it is not shining;
In love even when I am alone;
and in God even when He is silent."

*Inscription found scratched into a wall
by someone hiding from Nazis.*

**Life happens to everyone. It's what you do when life happens that reveals your character.
In times of crisis, we demonstrate our character.**

8
FLOUR & DOUGH

Our real battle is not about having vision, but maintaining it. It's in keeping the momentum and intensity for what we know God desires us to do. The weeks, months, and even years of battles go by. We get so weary at times it can appear the enemy is winning.

Life is as much about the journey as it is the destination. Our focus ought not to be on our battles, but on Jesus. Life happens when we are busy planning something else. One day in the plan and will of God can change everything. The cross had the appearance of failure. After the cross, the multitude of followers were reduced to 120 committed and faithful.

What a difference one day can make when God steps onto the scene! In less than 24 hours, the 120 exploded and multiplied into 3,120! The lesson here is to keep going. Keep on walking with Jesus, no matter what.

Life is as much about the journey as it is the destination.

WILL I SURVIVE?

Purpose and Destiny

I am writing to someone who senses destiny on their life and who believes God has a divine purpose for them. You have a dream and it won't let go. Words such as "purpose" and "destiny" speak of a higher calling, some greater meaning beyond your life itself. You have faced what you have gone through because there is something greater in store. The best is yet to come!

The scriptures are full of individuals who remained faithful and kept on going. History is full of faithful people as well. You know the story of their glory, but they had their moments of doubt and hardship too.

In 1954, Jimmy Denny, manager of the Grand Ole Opry, fired Elvis Presley after one performance. He told Elvis, "You ain't going nowhere, son. You ought to go back to driving a truck." But Elvis had a sense of purpose and destiny burning in his soul. He ignored the negativity and keep on going.

When Alexander Graham Bell invented the telephone in 1876, it didn't exactly ring off the hook with calls from potential backers. After making a demonstration call, President Rutherford B. Hayes said, "That's an amazing invention, but who would ever want to use one of them?"

Can you believe this... the schoolteachers in Michigan complained that Thomas Edison was "too slow" and hard to handle. As a result, Edison's mother decided to take her son out of school and teach him at home. Oh, and by the way, in his lifetime, Edison produced more than

FLOUR & DOUGH

1,300 inventions. Wouldn't it be great if more mothers took this same approach and gave their intelligent children the opportunity to excel in their strengths?

Lucille Ball began studying to be an actress in 1927. The head instructor of the John Murray Anderson Drama School told her, "Try any other profession. Any other."

In 1944, Emmeline Snively, director of the Blue Book Modeling Agency, told Marilyn Monroe, "You'd better learn secretarial work, or else get married."

Others May, I May Not

Are you familiar with the saying, "When the going gets tough, the tough get going"? As the baby is ready to be born, it will feel more restricted. As you become Christ-like, you will feel more restrictions.

The man Christ Jesus could not do what He wanted. His focus was to do the will of His Father. Likewise, as you become more like Him, your calling, destiny and sense of purpose will automatically give you the mindset, "Others may, but I may not."

That is to say, I have the Spirit and the hand of the Lord on me; therefore, what others may do, I may not. I have a higher sense of calling and belonging. I must be about my Master's business. I have chosen and have submitted myself to His purpose and process in life. I am not my own. I have been bought with a price and now I want to live, glorify and praise Jesus.

WILL I SURVIVE?

Keep Your Heart

The main thing is to keep the main thing, the main thing. Your life source is your heart. I'm not talking about a muscle that beats blood. I'm talking about your heart and soul, the place from which all the issues of life flow.

> *Keep your heart with all diligence, for out of it spring the issues of life.*
> **Proverbs 4:23**

Keep your heart. Guard it; protect it; maintain it; obey it. Daily living has a way of trying to burden and taint your heart. Life will take its toll and detour you. Then again, there is the enemy of your soul whose only purpose is to steal, kill and destroy (John 10:10).

If you do not keep your heart, it will not keep you focused on God's purpose and process. Heart disease can be congenital; you can be born with it. There are generational flows and curses. So we remain at the altar and keep an attitude of humility before our Creator (James 4:10).

Heart disease can also be acquired; gained through life's hard circumstances and situations. Is heart disease a part of the process? Here we must, for our calling and destiny sake, learn to live in love and forgiveness. We must embrace our place, not allowing any of these "things" to move us off God's course of conforming us into His image.

FLOUR & DOUGH

The Change From Wheat to Flour

You do not make bread out of wheat grain. A change has to take place in the wheat before it can make bread; it must be transformed into flour. When God is ready to use us, He reaches into the void of storage and takes out a measure of grain and puts it into the mill. He begins to grind the grain between two stones. The outer shell is crushed and ground until it is no longer identifiable.

All individual self-identity, which separates me from you, and you from me, must be eliminated before we can become bread. God will grind and grind us, until all flesh is gone and we become one in unity. That is, it's not all about "me" anymore.

> **A gem cannot be polished without friction, nor a man perfected without trials.**
> **-Lucius Seneca**

It is during the grinding process that something truly transforming takes place. Now grain is no longer called wheat anymore. It has a new identity; it has a new name. Now it is called flour.

Coarse flour was more commonly used in everyday life than fine flour, as there was less time involved in the grinding process. Still, all the bread in the temple was made of fine flour. God's bread, the church body of Christ, is made of fine flour, which involves more time in the process.

Have you ever felt as if you were between a rock and a hard place? ***Good news, God has you right where He needs you. He is getting ready to use you for His***

WILL I SURVIVE?

kingdom's purpose and glory!

Somewhere between the rock of Gethsemane and the rock of Golgotha, you and I are being ground. The process continues until the individual "I" ceases to exist. I become one with my brethren, and we become the flour of the body of Christ.

Motive

That no flesh should glory in His presence. 1 Cor. 1:29

To God, intent and motive are very important. The word "glory" here means to boast. Therefore, if I am glorying in God's presence I'm using Him to affect people's opinion of me. I'm using the Lord's anointing to draw attention to me.

Selfless and true ministry is God using you to affect people's opinion of Him. Selfish and false ministry is you using God to affect people's opinion of you. If you use God to gain friends or influence, you are glorying in His presence, and you won't make it with that kind attitude.

Flour is not Bread

At this point the wheat has become flour, but flour is not bread. Some make bread by simply adding water to the flour, but the best bread is made by also pouring in oil.

True ministry is God using you to affect people's opinion of HIM.

FLOUR & DOUGH

In scripture, oil represents the Holy Spirit of God.

As you and I stop jostling for position and glory, and lose our identities by being ground and mixed with each other, the Lord pours in His Spirit. After the outer shells are gone and our individual identities are ground and crushed away, God pours Himself—the oil—into the flour. The hand of God kneads us and mixes us together. Then He mixes Himself in when our identities no longer separate from each other.

> *I have been crucified with Christ; it is no longer I who live, but Christ lives in me; and the life which I now live in the flesh I live by faith in the Son of God, who loved me and gave Himself for me.*
> **Galatians 2:20**

Life is no longer about me; it is all about Him. The hand of God mixes us—flour, water, and oil—until we are something altogether different. We are no longer called flour, but dough. You, and I, and God are one together.

Dough is not Bread

We are so close, but still dough is not bread. Now is the time to take the dough and put it in the oven. Here, all the chaff—all the slander, accusations, bad talk—comes in to turn the heat up. But this time, we are not in the fire alone. We have the vast Body of Christ and the Spirit of

WILL I SURVIVE?

God there with us.

Are you ready for this next part? It is in the fire that dough is transformed into bread. We cannot escape, or run from the fire. We need the fire! It is an essential part of the process. After we come through the fire, we as bread can feed the hungry world.

> *And as they were eating, Jesus took bread, blessed and broke it, and gave it to the disciples and said, "Take, eat; this is My body."*
> **Matthew 26:26**

Is it all done yet? Well, yes and no. Yes, you are a part of the bread. There is nothing quite like fresh bread. It is so very good! The first thing Jesus does when you come out of the fire is He blesses you. And you are blessed! You are hand-chosen of the Lord.

The Word continues to say Jesus took, blessed, broke, and gave the bread. After blessing, He broke it? Yes. He takes you and blesses you; next, He breaks you in order to multiply and use you for His purpose.

> *Then He commanded the multitudes to sit down on the grass. And He took the five loaves and the two fish, and looking up to heaven, He blessed and broke and gave the loaves to the disciples; and the disciples gave to the multitudes.*
> **Matthew 14:19**

FLOUR & DOUGH

With sanctified blessed bread, He feeds a hungry world. *"Take, eat, this is My body."* Don't be angry with God when you go through one of the bread-making, bread-blessing, or bread-breaking stages. Don't be frustrated or kick against God because you are in the process. **The process proves you are wheat and not tares or chaff.** Be thankful, as you are still part of His plan. You're right on schedule.

Here is a great promise, *"Being confident of this very thing, that He who has begun a good work in you will complete it until the day of Jesus Christ"* (Philippians 1:6).

God will do His part if you do yours. That is to say, God will not stop or quit on you as long as you don't abort, or stop working with Him. The phrase "will complete" means to carry it on to completion, to fulfill, to complete entirely.

Don't bail out of the process. God will not stop working with you to bring you into your destiny. Do your part and stay with it.

The LORD is with you while you are with Him. If you seek Him, He will be found by you; but if you forsake Him, He will forsake you.
2 Chronicles 15:2

With every promise God gives, there is always a condition. Check it out. God says He'll do this, if you do that. His promises are fulfilled if we meet the

WILL I SURVIVE?

requirement. There is always a free-will choice involved in the equation. God will not force or make you do anything. That is why it is so very imperative we walk humbly and circumspectly before Him. It's not over till it's over.

> *Therefore, my dear friends, as you have always obeyed, not only in my presence, but now much more in my absence, continue to work out your salvation with fear and trembling . . .*
> **Philippians 2:12 NIV**

God is in the process. More importantly, He is with you in the process. For the child of God, everything is always okay in the end. If it's not okay, then it's not the end yet (Romans 8.28).

SURVIVING & THRIVING

9
LIVING IN TWO PLACES

Really? How is it possible to live in two places at the same time? It sounds a little confusing at first. In the natural it would be an almost schizophrenic experience. It would be as if you were neither here, nor there, yet you were both places. Despite what appears unhealthy and impossible, I am suggesting it is not only possible to live in two places at once, but necessary in order to learn and grow spiritually, mentally and emotionally.

By now you know bad things happen to good people and good things happen to bad people. This does not mean bad people are good, nor does it mean good people are bad, in spite of what occurs in their lives. If you are going to survive walking through this world of sin and live with God, you will need to keep your eyes on Jesus and develop the art of living in two places at the same time. Jesus made it very clear when He said, in this world you **will** have trouble, pressure and affliction. Yet at the same time, we are to have great courage.

These things I have spoken to you, that in Me you may have peace. In the world you will have tribulation, but

WILL I SURVIVE?

be of good cheer; I have overcome the world.
John 16:33

Living in the Wilderness

The Bible tells us Jesus went into the wilderness "full of the Holy Spirit" (Luke 4:1). Matter-a-fact, it is quite clear He was "led up by the Spirit into the wilderness" (Matthew 4:1). The wilderness then was a God-thing, God directed, God lead, God ordained. After going through His temptations, trials and tribulations, the Bible says Jesus came out of the wilderness in the **power** of the Spirit.

The word for power in the Greek is *dunamas*, which is where we get our English word dynamite. If you dig a little deeper, the root meaning is the inherited ability, or the miraculous power to do. Notice the 'dynamite' anointing or truly the 'power to do' came **after** the wilderness experience, after He had gone through a very strenuous spiritual, mental, emotional and physical time period. See what happens when you stay in the process?

The 'dynamite' anointing or truly the 'power to do' came after the wilderness experience.

After Jesus fasted forty days and forty nights, the tempter came and encouraged Him to turn stones into bread (Matthew 4:2-3). At that very moment Jesus was physically vulnerable. Hunger is not a sin. So, what's the big deal here?

The challenge from the enemy of your soul is this:

LIVING IN TWO PLACES

you belong to God and the power of God is in you. Right now you are in a stressful and difficult place. Why not use the power of God you have and deliver yourself? After all, why have power if you're not going to use it?

Knowing you have power with God to deliver yourself is one of the most deceptive temptations you will face. You have passion for God, and you are committed and surrendered. If the Lord leads, or allows you to go into a wilderness experience it won't be long before you will begin to have some questions. You will begin to lose your bearing and start wondering about God's purpose for your life. While you pray, the adversary comes and plants seeds of doubt and paranoia. The enemy wants you to act independently of the Father. He wants you to think your apparent "suffering" is not of God. You do not have to go through this. You have the power of God in you, so use it. Speak the word and free yourself. Satisfy your own hunger. Temptation rages within.

Do with me as You will; spend me as You wish.

Do you see what will happen if you fall into this temptation? You will try praying yourself out of what God has led you into, and nothing will happen. Because your wilderness is a God-thing, you are not going to obtain your desired answer from God, and you will begin questioning yourself **and** God. With doubt planted in your mind, you will progress into questioning your eternal purpose and if this process is real, or even worth it.

WILL I SURVIVE?

Jesus, our example, made it very clear He could not do anything in and of Himself. He restricted and confined His ministry to two areas: (1) I only do what I **see** my Father do, and (2) I only say what I **hear** my Father say.

Then Jesus answered and said to them, "Most assuredly, I say to you, the Son can do nothing of Himself, but what He sees the Father do; for whatever He does, the Son also does in like manner. I can of Myself do nothing. As I hear, I judge; and My judgment is righteous, because I do not seek My own will but the will of the Father who sent Me."
John 5:19, 30

"For I have not spoken on My own authority; but the Father who sent Me gave Me a command, what I should say and what I should speak. And I know that His command is everlasting life. Therefore, whatever I speak, just as the Father has told Me, so I speak."
John 12:49-50

How much more ought we to restrict ourselves to only do what we see the Father doing, and only say what we hear the Father saying. This of course implies the absolute necessity of having eyes to see and ears to hear. The whole subject will need more space and time than we have in this book. Still, this is a good place to start: "Jesus, open my eyes to see and my ears to hear."

LIVING IN TWO PLACES

If you live for God, then satan's aim and goal is for you to learn to disobey God for your own well-being. The enemy wants you to use the power God gave you against God's own will. Use it to avoid suffering and maybe later, you will use it to avoid the cross.

Even at the height of Jesus' suffering, He did not lose sight of the eternal purpose and process in life. He resisted the temptation to use God's power and anointing to save Himself. His focus and reply was simply, "It is written."

> **Jesus restricted His ministry to two areas:**
> **(1) He would only do what He sees His Father do.**
> **(2) He would only say what He heard His Father say.**

But He answered and said, "It is written, 'Man shall not live by bread alone, but by every word that proceeds from the mouth of God.'"
Matthew 4:4

In essence Jesus, the man, was saying it is not all about me. My time on earth is not centered around my needs, hurts or physical comfort. I am here to do the will and pleasure of the Father. **Do with me as You will; spend me as You wish.** I am not my own; I am all Yours.

Wrong Source

One of my favorite verses is John 10:10. If you remember

WILL I SURVIVE?

this one verse, it can be a great source of understanding and comfort.

> *The thief does not come except to steal, and to kill, and to destroy. I have come that they may have life, and that they may have it more abundantly.*
> **John 10:10**

Not only is the devil a liar, but he is also a thief. His main mission is to steal, kill and destroy everything you are and everything you have. Jesus' main mission is to bring you life, but not just ordinary everyday kind of living. His life, His Spirit in you is the beginning of abundant life. That's superior and superabundant. Of course that's if you let Him be formed in you.

Jesus is the only source of abundant life. If He is not your source, then something else will fill the void. Far too frequently your close association with the world may easily confuse you and cause you to compare and lean on another source for what may feel like "abundant" living. You **must** keep and maintain your life focus on Jesus as the author and finisher of your faith and life (Hebrews 12:2).

> *. . . Don't you know that friendship with the world is hatred toward God? Anyone who chooses to be a friend of the world becomes an enemy of God.*
> **James 4:4 NIV**

LIVING IN TWO PLACES

The sinful mind is hostile to God. It does not submit to God's law, nor can it do so. Those controlled by the sinful nature cannot please God.
Romans 8:6-8 NIV

If you believe all things work together for the good of those that love God, then He brought you to a place to bring you into the next place. God is in what you are going through. If you continue in the process and allow Him to be formed in you, things will work out for good, in time, all the time.

. . . All things work together for good to those who love God, to those who are the called according to His purpose. For whom He foreknew, He also predestined to be conformed to the image of His Son, that He might be the firstborn among many brethren.
Romans 8:28-30

John

Remember John the Beloved, the disciple of Jesus? He learned to live in two places at the same time. They horribly tormented and persecuted him by trying to boil him in oil. That has got to hurt! After they judged and rejected him, they abandoned and banished him to the desert and barren Island of Patmos.

How would you feel about living for God if you went through what John went through? You would probably

WILL I SURVIVE?

experience major feelings of rejection and loneliness. Most certainly, you would struggle with discouragement and bouts of depression. Not only would you be filled with physical pain, but mental and emotional anguish would be excruciating. Spiritually, most would honestly be overwhelmed with questions as to the sovereignty and love of God. Where is He? And why is He allowing all of this to happen to me?

Yet, John learned to live in two places. Outwardly it was very bleak, disastrous and hopeless. But inwardly, he maintained his strength, confidence and love for God. In the middle of his enormous crisis, John wrote the Book of Revelation. Look at the attitude and the words he used at the beginning of his writing:

> *I, John, both your brother and companion in the tribulation and kingdom and patience of Jesus Christ, was on the island that is called Patmos for the word of God and for the testimony of Jesus Christ.* ***I was in the Spirit*** *on the Lord's Day, and I heard behind me a loud voice, as of a trumpet...*
> ***Revelation 1:9-10***

Right in the middle of John's life threatening crisis and darkest nightmare, he is caring for, and reaching out to the family of God. If you are going to be in the Spirit, that means you have chosen not to be in the flesh. You can't have it both ways. If you can get past your situation and circumstances and manage to get into the Spirit of

LIVING IN TWO PLACES

God, you will begin hearing what the Spirit is saying.

I guarantee the Spirit of God is not worried, concerned or fearful of what's happening in our world. So if you manage to get into the Spirit, you will begin hearing spiritual things from God. And what do you suppose you'll hear?

In scripture, the trumpet is most commonly used as a symbol of victory. This means if you can live in two places and manage to have faith in God and get into the Spirit in the middle of your dark times, you will begin hearing what the Spirit is saying and not what your fear and doubt is screaming at you. As a result, you will always shout the victory, no matter what comes your way!

Jonah

Here's a man with a mission, and the call of God on his life. God speaks and directs him to take a message to the city of Nineveh. Jonah is overcome with nervous fear and runs the other way. In his attempt to get away from God's will, he relinquishes himself towards suicide and is tossed into the ocean and subsequently a whale swallows him.

I think wanting to end your life and being swallowed by a whale is a major life crisis; don't you? And being in the belly of a whale, I would think Jonah had a real problem focusing on anything outside of half-digested sea-weed and rotting fish. Can you relate to what it is like living in a really bad, awful and desperate place?

WILL I SURVIVE?

In a physically, mentally and emotionally catastrophic atmosphere, Jonah learned the art of living in two places. While in the belly of a whale, look at what he said and what happened to him at quite literally the lowest time of his life:

**He brought you to a place,
to bring you into the next place.**

But I will sacrifice to You, With the voice of thanksgiving; I will pay what I have vowed. Salvation is of the LORD. So the LORD spoke to the fish, and it vomited Jonah onto dry land.
Jonah 2:9-10

Honestly, who is thinking about much less wanting to offer up thanksgiving to God while living at rock bottom? Still, Jonah remembered his vow and commitment to God. You made a commitment to God when you were in your right mind, and that commitment was not just for the good times.

Anyone can offer thanksgiving and praise to God when things are going well. Jonah said, "I will sacrifice." You have the power to choose every day. A sacrifice is something you don't really feel like doing. "Choose you this day whom ye will serve" (Joshua 24:15) and where you want to live.

The Joy of the Lord is your strength.

LIVING IN TWO PLACES

Paul and Silas

Then of course there is the familiar example of Paul and Silas. Here are two men of God doing the work of God. Imagine doing the will of God and being mistreated. That never happens! (I wish!)

Paul and Silas were very wrongly accused and brutally beaten. They were manhandled and unjustly thrown into prison. Remember, in those days prisons were certainly no picnic.

If anyone had a right to have an attitude and be depressed, it was these two guys. I mean where's God when you need Him? If I'm doing God's will, shouldn't everything go smoothly?

Their story is a great example of being able to live in two places at the same time. So in this very damp, dingy, disgusting dilemma, at their darkest hour, what are they to do? Paul and Silas **chose** to worship and glorify God.

But at midnight Paul and Silas were praying and singing hymns to God . . . Suddenly there was a great earthquake . . . and immediately all the doors were opened and everyone's chains were loosed.
Acts 16:25-27

Again, who honestly feels like singing after being mistreated, beaten and unjustly thrown into a dungeon? Paul and Silas knew the value and power of keeping their eyes on Jesus and not on the circumstances. Over months

WILL I SURVIVE?

and years they learned there is great power and anointing released in the sacrifice of worship.

> *Let the saints be joyful in glory ... Let the high praises of God be in their mouth, And a two-edged sword in their hand, To execute vengeance on the nations, And punishments on the peoples; To bind their kings with chains, And their nobles with fetters of iron; To execute on them the written judgment – This honor have all His saints. Praise the LORD!*
> **Psalm 149:5-9**

Where do you live? I cannot over state this fact: if you are going to survive walking through this world of sin and live with God, you will need to keep your eyes on Jesus and develop the art of living in two places at the same time. Don't you think it's time to walk in the full Son-light? Only the Lord Jesus has abundant life to offer. Why not live to the fullest, with Him?

10
RELEASING THE MIRACLE

I want to tell you how to release the miracle God has for your life. Before I do, I want to say it is tragic when we become paralyzed by fear of failure or rejection. Before you take one step forward, before you even try to see what's possible, you will quit because you don't want to face failure or rejection.

Babe Ruth

I open this chapter with the story of the legendary home run king Babe Ruth. He was the first player to hit 60 home runs in one season. Some say baseball became popular only after Babe Ruth started playing in the 1920s.

When you think of Babe Ruth, you don't think of failure. But get this, from 1926 until 1964 Babe Ruth held the Major League Baseball career strikeout record! He swung at a lot of pitches and didn't hit the ball for most of them. The very area he failed in is what ended up making him a success.

The very area Babe Ruth failed in is what ended up making him a success.

Fear levels the playing field. If

WILL I SURVIVE?

you can handle fear and rejection, you'll become part of a small fraternity of dreamers who see their ideas become reality. After you make it past your first few rejections, the field of dreamers begins to quickly thin out.

We must become people who are not only familiar with fear, but also at ease with rejection as we pursue our calling before God. We've got to stop letting fear and rejection deter us.

As an analogy, think about how Westerners feel about the bartering system of some other cultures. Most people are crushed by the fear of rejection when it comes to asking for a lower price.

When I first moved to Hong Kong, bartering was awkward until I understood it is the way of life there. After time and a little practice, some of my Chinese friends couldn't believe the prices I was getting, all as a result of accepting rejection as part of the cultural game.

It's not what you know, but what you do with what you know.

You must press through fear and past rejection as God opens some doors and closes others. It's all a part of the process of learning and growing. The only way to find God's blessing for your life is by sifting through fear and rejection.

There will always be some amount of fear as you step up to the plate in the journey of life, but to hit a home run you have to persevere. You have to keep trying. Keep swinging. When you press through your fear, when you maneuver around rejection, something amazing happens:

eventually, you will get a hit! And your blessing becomes one step closer to reality.

Jesus talked about taking a bold step forward and acting out of belief. You see there is a vast difference between confessing Jesus as Lord, and making Jesus Lord.

"But why do you call Me 'Lord, Lord,' and not do the things which I say? Whoever comes to Me, and hears My sayings and does them, I will show you whom he is like: He is like a man building a house, who dug deep and laid the foundation on the rock. And when the flood arose, the stream beat vehemently against that house, and could not shake it, for it was founded on the rock. But he who heard and did nothing is like a man who built a house on the earth without a foundation, against which the stream beat vehemently; and immediately it fell. And the ruin of that house was great."
Luke 6:46-49

Physical growth is a process of **time**. Intellectual growth is a process of **learning**. Spiritual growth is not about time or learning, but it is the direct result of learning **obedience** time after time!

In one of the churches I pastored, I had a 3D sign made. It read, *"If I'm teachable, I'm fixable."* It matters not to God your background, education, talent, or lack thereof. What matters is, are you teachable? The key factor here is willingness on your part. One of the key elements in willingness is repentance, or submission to God's way, which is a matter of will. You see, repentance brings the God-Factor into play.

> *For rebellion is as the sin of witchcraft, And stubbornness is as iniquity and idolatry. Because you have rejected the word of the LORD, He also has rejected you from being king.*
> **1 Samuel 15:23**

In the original Hebrew, the message becomes even clearer, as the Word states flat out: "rebellion **is** witchcraft." The majority of times, when you see defiance or unwillingness played out, it is coming from a spirit of witchcraft at work. It stems from a refusal to accept some type of authority in a person's life. For a believer, the authority is the Spirit and Word of God.

> **Physical growth is a process of time.**
> **Intellectual growth is a process of learning.**
> **Spiritual growth is not about time or learning,**
> **but it is the direct result of learning obedience**
> **time after time!**

What is sin?

While it is possible to come up with a good number of definitions of sin, 1 John 3:4 spells it out rather succinctly:

RELEASING THE MIRACLE

"sin is lawlessness" (NIV). The root word used is "iniquity" with the intended meaning of *"no rule."* Sin is not having any rule or authority in your life. Without God's plumb line, your own fallen deprived nature is the only thing at work.

> *Because the carnal mind is enmity against God; for it is not subject to the law of God, nor indeed can be.*
> **Romans 8:7**

Let's be very clear here. Satan's demise was a direct result of his rejection to submit to the rule and reign of the Lord God. It was rejection and defiance that sent him hurling out of Heaven. It is the same spirit of rejection and lack of surrender to God that will keep you and I out of Heaven as well.

> *For you (Lucifer) have said in your heart: 'I will ascend into heaven, I will exalt my throne above the stars of God; I will also sit on the mount of the congregation on the farthest sides of the north; I will ascend above the heights of the clouds, I will be like the Most High.' Yet you shall be brought down to Sheol, To the lowest depths of the Pit.*
> **Isaiah 14:13-15**

WILL I SURVIVE?

The Power of Choice

Let's go back to the book of beginnings when God created Adam and Eve. God gave them great freedom and liberty. So what was His purpose putting a tree in the middle of the garden and then saying, *don't pick the fruit?* In hindsight, it would have been a whole lot easier not to have the tree in the garden in the first place.

God didn't put the tree there to test the first man and woman, as much He put it there to give humanity the ability to freely choose. You see, God did not make or want robots. He made mankind specifically with the freedom of choice. So with one act of disobedience, sin entered the world and separated mankind from God.

You and I were specifically created to have fellowship with Almighty God. We have, if you please, a built in Jesus hole and no matter how hard we try, nothing will fill and satisfy that need, except for the One True God of the Bible.

If an act of disobedience separates us from God, what do you think would connect us back into relationship with Him? Obedience. Obedience is expressed by our ability to choose and submit to God's rule and authority.

So to mankind, the message is rather quite simple: choose life and live.

> *I call heaven and earth as witnesses today against you, that I have set before you life and death, blessing and cursing; therefore choose life, that both you and your*

RELEASING THE MIRACLE

descendants may live; that you may love the LORD your God, that you may obey His voice, and that you may cling to Him, for He is your life and the length of your days...
Deuteronomy 30:19-20

And if it seems evil to you to serve the LORD, choose for yourselves this day whom you will serve, whether the gods which your fathers served that were on the other side of the River, or the gods of the Amorites, in whose land you dwell. But as for me and my house, we will serve the LORD."
Joshua 24:15

Your free choice is your greatest gift and your greatest curse. Without repentance and turning to the God of the Bible, you will perish. *"I tell you, no; but unless you repent you will all likewise perish"* (Luke 13:3).

That at the name of Jesus every knee should bow, of those in heaven, and of those on earth, and of those under the earth, and that every tongue should confess that Jesus Christ is Lord, to the glory of God the Father.
Philippians 2:10-11

Let's go back to the scripture verse in the Book of Samuel we first read, as it sheds further revelation on this subject.

WILL I SURVIVE?

For rebellion is as the sin of witchcraft, And stubbornness is as iniquity and idolatry. Because you have rejected the word of the LORD, He also has rejected you from being king.
1 Samuel 15:23

Notice in this verse that along with rebellion, stubbornness is mentioned. Again, the Hebrew is far clearer which says, *"Stubbornness is iniquity and idolatry."* The Bible is telling us stubbornness is the refusal to have God's rule in your life. Stubbornness is being unyielding, obstinate and inflexible when it comes to God's Word. If you are stubborn, you are an idolater—one serving and submitted to another god. Self, money, sex, positions, mother earth… You make a god out of whatever you want to.

Be It Unto Me

God wants to release a miracle in your life. In order for this to take place, we need to look at a great life revelation from Mary, the mother of Jesus.

Now in the sixth month the angel Gabriel was sent by God to a city of Galilee named Nazareth, to a virgin betrothed to a man whose name was Joseph, of the house of David. The virgin's name was Mary. And having come in, the angel said to her, "Rejoice, highly favored one, the Lord is with you; blessed are

RELEASING THE MIRACLE

This is a really powerful verse. Notice the verse starts with "**and**," which is a conjunction word bringing together the part before and the part to follow.

"With God nothing will be impossible." As powerful as the statement is, the whole thought is not complete. Scripture goes on to complete the intended thought and revelation.

You would think that after a proclamation and announcement of God's intended will, it would all be over. I mean, this is God's will we're talking about. This is God's plan, right? Just wait one minute. Can anyone show me in scripture where God ever crosses human will? Remember, we are not robots. It was God's idea to give humanity free choice.

I will suggest to you Mary was **not** pregnant **until** she said, "be it unto me." She expressed her willingness to submit herself to the Lord God's rule and plan. There was no resistance, no defiance, no rebellion or thought of self. When God spoke, she simply complied with, *"be it unto me."*

There's still another *"and"* in the verse, suggesting the intended thought is still not over. "*And* the angel departed." There's the conjunction word again. Even though the will of God was expressed, the angel had to wait and see if Mary would comply and be a willing participant. Then, and only then, could he leave.

Mary was not pregnant until she said, "be it unto me."

WILL I SURVIVE?

Home Visitation

Upon arrival at one of the churches I pastored, I made an effort to visit the homes of each church member. One senior lady, whose husband did not attend services, made arrangements for me to come to their home for tea.

After introductions were made, the husband, being the no-nonsense type he was, asked what I was doing there. I explained that as the new pastor in town, I wanted to meet with each church member in their homes. He proceeded to articulate very clearly he was not interested in church, the Bible, or God. He said if I wanted to talk about any of that "stuff," I was not welcome and should leave now. I replied I was quite capable of talking about a good number of subjects, including, but not limited to the weather!

The husband ended up telling stories of his involvement in back room politics. I actually enjoyed our visits and learned a great deal about the ins and outs of government. Over a number of years, I visited the home a few times. Again and again, he made it very clear I was not to bring up or talk about God or the Bible. Did I mention the man had ALS, Lou Gehrig's disease, and was dying a slow death?

One day I had a night vision, a dream, about the man. As I awoke, I instantly knew the dream was God-sent. In my dream, the husband was lying in bed, frail and weak. As I drew near, the man's face and countenance was euphoric. He had one hand held up in the air and I saw

11
THE TWO HANDS OF GOD

While traveling as an Evangelist, the Lord held me in Arizona for three weeks with no preaching engagements. With beautiful weather and time on my hands, I enjoyed taking long walks. It was during one of my prayer and meditation walks with the Lord I felt Him whisper, *"The Left Hand, of God."*

I think I may have read or heard something about the left hand of God somewhere some time, but at that moment I was completely in the dark as to what it meant. Perplexed, somewhat intrigued, I

Have you ever heard of The Left Hand of God?

began my journey into revelation. Not only has understanding about the left hand of God impacted me, but I have shared my insight with multitudes bringing comfort and courage into their lives.

Attributes

Among the attributes of God, we know He is Omnipresent. God is everywhere present and nowhere absent. He fills all of space. At this very second, He is

WILL I SURVIVE?

with you. He is also in Asia, as well as Europe. There is no place in existence where God is not already there. As well as filling all space, God also fills all time. While God is literally here at the present moment, He is already in your tomorrow. Now stop and think about that one!

God is Omniscient. He knows **all** things. There simply is not one thing He does not know from your past, present or future. Plus, He is Omnipotent. He has all power and with Him, nothing is impossible.

In all of His power, knowledge and infinity, God still gives the human race the free will to choose. The Bible is very clear, God is not willing that any should perish (2 Peter 3:9). Still, each and every one of us is accountable for our own actions as we stand before our Maker. Your life choices will be the basis of your eternal destination, in light of His Word.

God is Spirit, and those who worship Him must worship in spirit and truth.
John 4:24

The Right Hand of God

Most may be familiar with, or at least have heard of the phrase, "the Right Hand of God." God is a Spirit and fills all space and time, so which side is right and which is left? For that matter, which way is up? As a Spirit, does God even have a hand? Hence the meaning of "the Right Hand of God" in scripture must be symbolic.

THE TWO HANDS OF GOD

Your right hand, O LORD, has become glorious in power; Your right hand, O LORD, has dashed the enemy in pieces.
Exodus 15:6

The Right Hand of God, in scripture, is a metaphor of His power and authority. The "Right Hand" is where God demonstrates His might, in miracles, signs and wonders!

The right hand of the LORD is exalted; the right hand of the LORD does valiantly.
Psalm 118:16

When Jesus was speaking to the High Priest in Matthew 26:64, He made this statement: *"...you will see the Son of Man sitting at the right hand of the Power, and coming on the clouds of heaven."* Now the book of Revelation is very clear, there is only one throne in heaven and Jesus is that One who is sitting on it (Revelation 4:2). Yet in Hebrews 12:2, we read Jesus *"is set down at the right hand of the throne of God."*

How do we harmonize the scriptures? You've heard the phrase, "my right hand man." Does it mean there is a person growing from or attached to your right hand? Of course not. It is a metaphor. In this case, it is a figure of speech used to describe the value and relationship of a person. Though God is a Spirit and does not literally have a right hand, He does have one symbolically, and

WILL I SURVIVE?

that right hand represents His power and authority.

In reality, it is the "demonstration hand" of God. It is how He expresses Himself.

The right hand of God represents His power and authority. It is where God demonstrates His might in miracles, signs and wonders.

...In Your presence is fullness of joy; at Your right hand are pleasures forevermore. **Psalm 16:11**

I have set the LORD always before me; because He is at my right hand I shall not be moved.
Psalm 16:8

Show Your marvelous loving kindness by Your right hand, O You who save those who trust in You...
Psalm 17:7

Your arm is endued with power; your hand is strong, your right hand exalted. **Psalm 89:13**

A thousand may fall at your side, and ten thousand at your right hand...
Psalm 91:7

Oh, sing to the LORD a new song! For He has done marvelous things; His right hand and His holy arm have gained Him the victory.
Psalm 98:1

THE TWO HANDS OF GOD

I love to see the Right Hand of Power express itself in all its might! Who wouldn't? Just last month I saw a tumor disappear. I can't begin to count the many personal healings and deliverances I've been honored to behold.

In one church, a member called the church asking for help. She needed someone to assist her into the car and into church, as she was in so much pain. In the service, God touched her body and she was instantly healed! Several days later, the Pastor mentioned to me the woman called him the next day still rejoicing from her complete healing! It is with the Right Hand of God where we shout, rejoice and testify as to what **He** has done!

The Bible says the Ten Commandments were written *"with the finger of God"* (Exodus 31:18). Does that mean God literally has a finger? No. The Bible uses the human body to metaphorically express attributes of God. Perhaps the finger of God represents what God is pointing to, the details He wants us to focus on. We already learned the Bible expresses God's power and might using the term *"right hand."* As humans, we are created in God's image, and we have two hands.

What does that tell us about God's *left hand?* What could it represent or symbolize?

God's Left Hand?

The Bible says very little about the *"Left Hand of God,"* but it does make reference to it. God is not one handed, nor is He limited to just one hand. He is in the truest sense ambidextrous—able to use both hands equally. The Book of Job refers to God's left hand when it says, *"the left hand, where He doeth work"* (Job 24:9 KJV). The New King James Version says it very plainly, *"He works on the left hand."*

The right hand in the Hebrew means stronger or more dexterous. And indeed, we do look to the Right Hand of God for the demonstration of power and might. On the other hand, no pun intended, left in Hebrew means "dark." The Latin word for left handed means, "sinister."

I am not suggesting God has a "dark" or "sinister" side, but there is a difference between God's use of His right hand and the use His left hand.

The Left and Right Side

Before I reveal the Left Hand of God, I would like to dispel another thought. It comes from Matthew 25:31-33.

> *When the Son of Man comes in His glory, and all the holy angels with Him, then He will sit on the throne of His glory. All the nations will be gathered before Him, and He will separate them one from another, as a shepherd divides his sheep from the goats. And He will set the sheep on His right hand, but the goats on the left.*
> ***Matthew 25:31-33***

THE TWO HANDS OF GOD

If, left means "dark" or "sinister," then please note that to move to the left side of the Judge, is a movement to the right of those facing him! The lesson in scripture is not one of a good side or bad side, but that there is a division. It is not about the side on which each group is placed.

God did not distinguish between left and right in 2 Chronicles 18:18 when it says, *"…Therefore hear the word of the Lord; I saw the Lord sitting upon His throne, and all the host of heaven standing on His right hand and on his left."* The Old Testament describes walking in God's will as turning *"neither to the right hand or to the left."*

> *Therefore you shall be careful to do as the LORD your God has commanded you; you shall not turn aside to the right hand or to the left.*
> **Deuteronomy 5:32**

The Left hand of God is not a negative, neither is it undesirable. The mother of disciples James and John requested and asked Jesus to seat her two sons *"one on Your right hand and the other on the left"* (Matthew 20:21).

Despite this equal use of the right and left hands, to conclude God is more dominate in one hand, the right hand, would not only be totally incorrect, but very restrictive, limited and short sighted. God is, in the truest sense, ambidextrous. He uses both hands equally.

WILL I SURVIVE?

Job of the Bible

In one tragic, dark, and terrible day, Job loses all of his children. His sons and daughters all die. He loses all of his cattle, sheep and livestock. He loses his livelihood. He loses all of his servants, all of his employees. He loses his camels, all of his transportation.

If that is not a bad enough day, his health fails completely, so he's hanging on to life by a thread. To top it off, his wife abandons him and his *"friends"* are fixated and determined to judge and condemn him with great zeal.

I don't know about you, but I've had some really bad, awful days. Still, I'm not sure if it quite compares to Job! The real kicker is this was all God's idea! (Job 1:8)
Then Job cries out these words, *"Look, I go forward, but He is not there…"* (Job 23:8).

It is terrifying when you can see no change in the horizon of your future. Comfort comes when we know current turbulence will soon be over. Yet where is the comfort when it seems as if problems will never cease? As a raging rainstorm that will not let up, the waters of discouragement begin to fill your tossing ship with water. Suddenly, you begin to experience a lonely, sinking feeling.

Have you ever been searching, praying, or crying out, and yet still feel you are getting no closer to your relief? *"Behold, I try to go forward … but He is not there …"*

Can you identify with the cartoon characters good

THE TWO HANDS OF GOD

old Charlie Brown and Linus? Both are standing outside under the vastness of the starry sky. Looking up, Charlie Brown comments, "Let's go inside. I am beginning to feel very insignificant." Have you ever felt that way, insignificant and unimportant? I have. And it's just a little overwhelming to say the least.

Comfort comes when we know current turbulence will soon be over.

". . . And backward, but I cannot perceive Him . . ." (Job 23:8).

Looking backward opens the door to hind-sight. Many times, with hindsight comes the opportunity for doubt and fear to grow. Our heart begins to fill with regret and second guessing.

The word "perceive" in this verse gives the idea of the inability to mentally distinguish or understand. *"Maybe I shouldn't have done that? Maybe I should have done it another way? Was that really God that I felt, speaking to me? I'm just not sure anymore. I don't understand what's going on. What's happening?"*

Without understanding the use of God's left hand, we will be thrown into discouragement and depression.

The Left Hand of God

On the left hand, where He doth work, but I cannot behold Him... Job 23:9 KJV

On the Right Hand of God is His authority and power-arm. It is where God demonstrates His might.

WILL I SURVIVE?

The Left Hand of God is where He is **still** at work. The word here gives the meaning of accomplishing or doing *"something."* Yes, God is at work, but we are clueless and cannot see what He's doing. *"I cannot behold Him."* I have no vision or understanding for what You are doing Lord, and I'm feeling lost!

> **. . . He hideth himself on the right hand, that I cannot see Him . . . Job 23:9**

Yes, God is working on the left hand, but when He is using His Left Hand, He is "hiding" or covering His Right Hand. *"I'm in a daze as I am not seeing Your Right Hand of power and might. Where are You, Lord?"* And without understanding, like Job, we are thrown for a major loop and fall into a tail spin, falling head long into some heavy-duty discouragement and depression. *"May the day perish on which I was born..."* (Job 3:3). Paraphrased: I wish I was never born! *"Why did I not die at birth? Why did I not perish when I came from the womb?"* (Job 3:11). Paraphrased: I wish I was dead! Why on earth, was I ever born? What's the purpose? Why am I even alive?

Depression

I'm not going to fill you up with statistics on depression, but I will give one. According to the Centers for Disease Control and Prevention and the National

THE TWO HANDS OF GOD

Institute of Mental Health, which is the largest scientific organization dedicated to mental health issues, the number of those diagnosed with depression increases by approximately 20 percent per year.

There are good people, even Bible believers who love God, that are lost in a vast ocean of despair and obscurity, overwhelmed with feelings of grave insignificance. Perhaps in our dark pit, we have forgotten and do not realize God is still sovereign! He is still in control! He is still supreme!

I do not remember where it came from. Perhaps from a book I read. I just remember the last line. At the end of it all: *"God is on His throne, and all is well."* So I remind myself in the middle of my dilemma. I audibly say it at the close of one of "those days" when it seems everything is awful. *"God is on His throne, and all is well."*

Yes, but nobody knows the trouble I've seen . . . Really? You really want to stick to that in light of Job's story? I could tell you some stories that would make your head spin. I'm sure you have a few of your own. Sometimes I wonder if I would believe my own stories if it were not for the fact that I've lived them!

God is on His throne, and all is well.

Let's talk about the only person described in scripture as a man after God's own heart. The Great King David, who, by-the-way was a man of great depression. *"Answer me when I call to you, [HELLO! Anyone there?]. Give me relief from my distress; be merciful to me and hear my prayer"* (Psalm 4:1 NIV).

WILL I SURVIVE?

Have mercy on me, O LORD, for I am weak; O LORD, heal me, for my bones are troubled. My soul also is greatly troubled; But You, O LORD — how long? Return, O LORD, deliver me! Oh, save me for Your mercies' sake! For in death there is no remembrance of You; In the grave who will give You thanks? I am weary with my groaning; All night I make my bed swim; I drench my couch with my tears.
Psalm 6:2-6

How long, O LORD? Will You forget me forever? How long will You hide Your face from me? How long shall I take counsel in my soul, Having sorrow in my heart daily? How long will my enemy be exalted over me? Consider and hear me, O LORD my God; Enlighten my eyes, Lest I sleep the sleep of death; Lest my enemy say, "I have prevailed against him." Lest those who trouble me rejoice when I am moved.
Psalm 13:1-4

Take a good look at Psalm 74:11 in the Amplified Bible. *"Why do You hold back Your hand, even Your right hand?"* I want to see Your right hand, oh God. I want to see the miraculous! I want to see *"something"* happening! I want to see You are doing *"something"* here!

Take a look at the strong and vigorous forerunner to Jesus. John the Baptist. He is a powerful man of God, a personal friend and cousin to Jesus. From a dungeon's

THE TWO HANDS OF GOD

hole in the ground he lifts his voice with hesitation. "Are you the one, or do I keep looking for another?" (Matthew 11:3)

After being in the darkness of despair for so long, John started questioning himself and his calling. *"I thought I knew, but I'm not sure anymore. Does this really work? Is this for real? Can I find deliverance from my anxiety? Can I fill this void in my life?"*

Behold, I go forward, but He is not there; and backward, but I cannot perceive Him: On the left hand, where He doth work, but I cannot behold Him: He hideth Himself on the right hand, that I cannot see Him . . .
Job 23:8,9 KJV

I am concerned and somewhat troubled for the church of today. It's a church that seems to always need entertainment and stimulation. Everything has to be smiles, fun and laughter. Real life is not like that. Don't get me wrong. I love to laugh and have a good time. But 24/7/365 is just not reality.

I remember going to the gym one winter's day. I spent a good amount of time on the treadmill and the elliptical trainer. It was hard not to view the rather large TV monitor on the wall right in front. Over the process of time, a number of different programs and talk shows played.

Everyone on TV was always smiling and happy!

WILL I SURVIVE?

I remember thinking, *"I wonder if we have allowed this false sense of entertainment to infiltrate the church?"* Have we reduced church to productions and performances? Have we made it a place where we are discouraged from being real and honest with each other, let alone ourselves? There seems to be a never-ending stimulation for emotional happiness and release.

The Jesus Genie

Then there is the idea of "Jesus the Genie." Remember Aladdin and the lamp? You find the old oil lamp hidden in the dark secret cave. It looks unique enough, so you pick it up and begin cleaning it. And as you rub away the dirt and grime, smoke begins to exit the lamp and in a matter of seconds, a Genie appears to grant you three magical wishes!

I know it's just a story, but that is how we treat the God of the Bible at times. We rush over to the Bible, pick it up and start rubbing it as we chant the words, "In Jesus Name! In Jesus Name! In Jesus Name!" Expecting, as if by some spiritual mystical magic, our very own personal *"Jesus Genie"* will do exactly what we tell Him.

Sounds far-fetched? Listen to your prayers some times.

Remember this: God displays His glory in the ashes of human frailty. For He works on the left hand! *". . . His strength is made perfect in weakness . . ."* (2 Corinthians 12:9). You can't see Him when He is working on the left

THE TWO HANDS OF GOD

hand. He is invisible over there. It appears that He is not there at all, but He is! Oh, yes, He is! And He is working. He is doing *"something."*

Okay, so here's where I'm going with this. The disciples were having a hard time trying to figure out the "whys" and "how comes" of life, as if life doesn't happen to everyone. Then Jesus dropped this golden nugget, *"Have faith in God."* More accurately, "Have the faith of God" (Mark 11:22).

The faith of God speaks to being fully persuaded of the truthfulness or credence of God. The root word means to be convicted. Do you have such a personal intimate relationship with your Creator that you just know that you know, and are secure in that knowledge?

So **when** things happen, you can remain unshaken and immoveable in your reliance, trust and confidence in the God who cares and said, *"I will never leave you nor forsake you"* (Hebrews 13:5). And, *"I am with you always, even to the end of the age"* (Matthew 28:20).

> **God displays His glory in
> the ashes of human frailty.**

The Brooklyn Bridge

For some reason the Brooklyn Bridge attracts hundreds of jumpers each year. Amazing enough, there are those who manage to survive. An interviewer spoke with numerous survivors and almost all felt great regret and

WILL I SURVIVE?

embarrassment at their choice. The conclusion: if they had waited just 24 hours, they would not have attempted suicide. What a difference one day makes!

Then the Lord directed my attention to Isaiah Chapter 45. There are multiple millions of believers today who do not like to believe that all things are of God, including evil. They much prefer to believe God created good and the devil created evil, but scripture says otherwise:

I am the LORD, and there is none else, there is no God beside me... That they may know from the rising of the sun, and from the west, that there is none beside me. I am the LORD, and there is none else. I form the light, and create darkness: I make peace, and create evil: I the LORD do all these things. **Isaiah 45:5-7 KJV**

**When things happen, remain unshaken
and immoveable in your reliance,
trust and confidence in the God who cares.**

After Isaiah states the fact there is only one God, he further clarifies the one true God is the source of light and revelation. The one true God also created darkness. The Hebrew gives greater insight to the meaning of darkness with such words as misery, sorrow, destruction and obscurity.

God makes peace, or the sense of tranquility, and *"creates evil."* The Hebrew for evil is, well, bad stuff. It denotes a fierceness of wilderness. Then, to keep it all in

THE TWO HANDS OF GOD

the right perspective the verse re-states and concludes, just in case you might have questions, *"I the LORD (Yahweh) do all these things."*

This whole portion of scripture affirms the absolute sovereignty of the LORD God. If that is not enough, verse 9 gives this warning:

Woe unto him that striveth with his Maker . . .
Isaiah 45:9 KJV

Just to drive this sovereignty thing further home, a strong suggestion is given to one that might *"strive"* with his Maker. Again, in the Hebrew, it becomes very clear with descriptive words such as don't grapple, wrangle, chide, complain, contend, or debate with God. In other words, don't fuss with God. You will lose.

Now, let's be very clear; the Bible plainly states God is love. He is good. He is life. Nowhere does the Bible say God is evil, only that He creates evil. There is a vast difference here. God uses just the right amount of situations and circumstances in our lives for His purpose. It is not even a question of how much God permits. Remember, God is supreme and sovereign. There is no one else beside Him (Isaiah 44:6, 8).

The Laws of Creation

One of the fundamental laws of creation is that an opposing force is necessary for growth in order to produce strength, stamina, and endurance. Any living thing that grows up without any opposition is weak and powerless.

God's new creation must be strong and powerful (2 Corinthians 5:17). Anyone who desires strength must wrestle and deal with a force contrary to them self. Any man who wants to develop muscular strength and power must spend weeks, months and perhaps years in vigorous training. Heavy exercise, lifting weights, and using the opposing force of gravity are all part of his development and routine.

A plant that grows in a greenhouse, sheltered from wind and rain, pampered day after day, may grow large, but it is inherently weak. If suddenly exposed to the elements it will wither and die. On the other hand, a plant constantly exposed to the fierce winds and pounding rains, burning heat and chilling cold, is strong and not easily destroyed.

Don't fuss with God. You will lose.

The Rock

I am reminded of a story. A man was sleeping one night in his cabin when suddenly his room filled with light, and God appeared. The Lord told the man he had a work for him to do, and revealed to him a large rock. The Lord explained that the man was to push against the rock with all of his might.

So, day after day, the man did just that. Weeks quickly

THE TWO HANDS OF GOD

passed into months and evolved into years. He toiled from sun up to sun down. His shoulders set squarely against the cold massive surface of the unmoving rock; he would push with all of his might. Each night, the man returned to his cabin sore and worn out, feeling his whole day was spent in vain.

Since the man was showing discouragement, the adversary, satan, decided to enter the picture by placing thoughts into his weary mind. "You have been pushing against that rock for a long time, and it hasn't moved." These thoughts gave the man the impression he was a failure and the task impossible.

He became discouraged and disheartened. "Why kill yourself over this? Just give the minimum effort and put in your time. Better still, why not go do something else that you want to do?"

The planted seeds grew within the weary man. In time, he decided he would quit. Almost an afterthought, the man decided to take his troubled thoughts to the Lord.

"Lord," he said, "I have labored long and hard in Your service, putting all my strength toward that which you have asked. Yet, after all of this time, I have not even budged the rock by half a millimeter. What's wrong with me? Why am I a failure?"

The Lord responded compassionately. "My friend, when I asked you to serve Me and you accepted, I told you your task was to push against the rock with all of your strength, which you have done. Never once did I say I expected you to move the rock. Your task was to push, and now you come to Me believing your strength is spent, and you have failed.

"Look at yourself. Your arms are strong and muscled, your back sinewy and brown; your hands are callused from constant pressure. Your legs have become massive and hard. Through opposition you have grown much, and your abilities now surpass that which you used to have.

"True, you haven't moved the rock, but your calling was to be obedient and to push and to exercise your faith, trusting My wisdom. You have done what I have called you to do. Now I will move the rock, so you can step into your destiny."

At times, when we hear a Word from God, we tend to use our own intellect to decipher what He wants, when actually what God wants is just simple obedience and confidence in Him.

So when everything seems to go wrong, keep pushing. When the money is gone and the bills are due, keep pushing. When people just don't understand you, keep pushing. When your task and calling gets you down, keep pushing.

Job's Lesson Conclusion

Behold, I go forward, but he is not there; and backward, but I cannot perceive him: On the left hand, where he doth work, but I cannot behold him:

THE TWO HANDS OF GOD

he hideth himself on the right hand, that I cannot see him . . .
Job 23:8, 9 KJV

But He knows the way that I take; when He has tested me, I shall come forth as gold.
Job 23:10

God is looking for simple obedience and confidence in Him.

Do you see it? Do you get it? You and I may not always know where we are, let alone where God is, but God knows. God sees. God cares. Jesus knows the exact road and course of life we take. If we continue in the process, after the trials and tests, we shall come out shining and shimmering as pure gold with His continued blessings.

The secret is to keep walking with the Lord Jesus, every day. It's that one on one personal intimate relationship with the One whom my soul loves. In His presence, with His understanding and comfort, we can live in perfect peace knowing He loves and cares for us individually and specifically. God is on His throne, and all is well.

But as it is written: "Eye has not seen, nor ear heard, Nor have entered into the heart of man the things which God has prepared for those who love Him." But God has revealed them to us through His Spirit.

WILL I SURVIVE?

For the Spirit searches all things, yes, the deep things of God.
1 Corinthians 2:9, 10

Look at the wording in this scripture:

Not that I speak in regard to need, for I have learned in whatever state [condition, or situation] I am, to be content: [absent of need, which means I'm not asking God to fix it]. I know how to be abased, and I know how to abound. Everywhere and in all things I have learned both to be full and to be hungry, both to abound and to suffer need. I can do all things through Christ who strengthens me.
Philippians 4:11-13

Grace

Jesus is the One who *strengthens me*. The grace of God gives strength. Grace is God's supernatural empowerment to do what you and I cannot do on our own. What are the "all things" I can do? I can be at *"peace"* in whatever state or situation I find myself. I can be content, absent of need. I can be full and empty at the same time. I can be abased, and abound at the same time.

Because Jesus is giving me the ability through His grace, I know my Father is in control. The devil did not put me in this situation. My Father allowed me to be in this situation for His plan and His purpose and I trust

THE TWO HANDS OF GOD

my Heavenly Father.

Therefore, I'm at peace in my situation for however long it lasts. If He wants me to pray about the situation, He will tell me what to pray, when to pray and how to pray because I'm not going to pray my way out of what God has allowed and put me in.

Great peace have they who love Your law; nothing shall offend them or make them stumble.
Psalm 119:165 AMP

My Heavenly Father is in control, and I trust Him.

Remember, *"he who endures to the end will be saved"* (Matthew 10:22). That is, he that stays under the purpose and process of God will be saved. Is that fatalism? No! It's called trust, based on a personal relationship with the Eternal Creator and Redeemer.

So do we then just give up and give in to everything? No! The only One I'm giving in to is my Lord and Savior. I'm giving up to His purpose and His process, because only He is sovereign and in control of all things, and He is caring for me.

Trust in the LORD with all your heart, and lean not [support not yourself] on Your own understanding.
Proverbs 3:5

WILL I SURVIVE?

Lean on, trust in, and be confident in the Lord with all your heart and mind and do not rely on your own insight or understanding.
Proverbs 3:5 AMP

My Lesson Conclusion

I need to finish the story I started at the beginning of this chapter. I was held captive and walking in beautiful sunny Arizona when the Lord began speaking to me about the Left Hand of God.

As the days passed and while He gave me revelation and understanding, I started to sing a song. I must have heard the song before, and maybe I don't have all the words right, but these are the words, which rolled over and over in my spirit. *"I believe, You're my Hero. I believe, You're more than enough for me."*

Day after day as I walked, I sang (or tried to), *"I believe, You're my Hero. I believe, You're more than enough for me."*

I thought, this must be a song out there somewhere, so I did a Google search and up popped the song by Mike Guglielmucci, "My Healer." I see now I had the words wrong, but I still prefer, "My Hero," as that is my attitude towards God through it all.

THE TWO HANDS OF GOD

My Healer

You hold my every moment,
You calm my raging seas
You walk with me through fire,
And heal all my disease

I trust in You (Lord), I trust in You

I believe You're my Healer
I believe You are all I need
I believe… I believe You're my portion
I believe You're more than enough for me
Jesus, You're all I need.

Nothing is impossible for You
Nothing is impossible
Nothing is impossible for You
You hold my world in Your hands

If that was not enjoyable enough, then the Lord directed me to the following scripture:

Heal me, O LORD, and I shall be healed; Save me, and I shall be saved: for You are my praise.
Jeremiah 17:14

WILL I SURVIVE?

What an attitude to have in life! Lord Jesus, if You heal me, I shall be healed. If You help me, I shall be helped. But whatever way it goes and however You see fit to direct it, You are my praise! You are my life!

You are my praise, Jesus

Philippians is possibly one of the last epistles Paul wrote while imprisoned in Rome after a life of great hardship and sacrifice. After all the beatings and stoning, the shipwrecks and many perils of hunger and thirst, together with the many infirmities, Paul penned these words:

Rejoice in the Lord always: Again I will say, rejoice!
Philippians 4:4

12
WHATSOEVER HE SAYS

God is more concerned about our character than our comfort. His goal is not to pamper us physically, but to perfect us spiritually. That being true, what does it say about the churches of today? Shouldn't that idea alone shed light on the spiritual direction of many? We certainly would not want to inconvenience anyone, or make them feel uncomfortable in the presence of God, now would we?

God is more concerned about your character than your comfort.

It has been my prayer that as you read this book you were met with revelation and understanding, and identified where you are in life's journey. In this last chapter, I would like to leave you with a life principle. If you keep this in mind, not only will you survive, you will thrive!

Let us hold fast the confession of our hope without wavering, for He who promised is faithful. And let us consider one another in order to stir up love and good works, not forsaking the assembling of ourselves

together, as is the manner of some, but exhorting one another, and so much the more as you see the Day approaching.
Hebrews 10:23-25

The intent behind the word *"stir up,"* or provoke in the KJV, gives the idea of sharpening by coming along side and exasperating, or irritating the individual to move or grow forward in their relationship with the Lord Jesus.

Today, if some church, preacher, or saint of God steps on our toes, not only may we never talk to them again, or attend their church, but we may be tempted to call down fire from Heaven. The very idea! Who do they think they are?

God uses our life circumstances and situations to mold, shape and direct our lives. He uses the difficulties of real life settings. Trust me, all places have some difficulty. God even uses the people He has allowed in our lives, both friends and foes, to help perfect us into His image. Remember, the pursuit of God is a primary step into worship. It's not about you.

The pursuit of God is a primary step into worship. It's not about you.

Saved By A No

Someone told me a story about a man in a church who wanted to work for a consulting team. He was confident he had the right credentials and work experience;

however, he did not get the assignment. He really wanted the job and could not understand for the life of him why he was denied the position.

His questioning stopped at 9:38 a.m., on September 11th when news sources reported American Airlines Flight 77 plunged into the west side of the Pentagon. All on board the plane and several on the ground were killed, including the entire consulting team this man would have been a member of **if** he had been given the job he wanted. A "No" answer saved his life. He was saved by not getting what he wanted.

We often say God "answered' our prayers when we receive what we want from Him. In reality a *"No,"* or *"Not Yet"* from God, is just as much an answer to prayer as a *"Yes"* is. Remember, God sees the end from the beginning and He may be saving you from a disaster.

Trust Him when you are unable to track Him.

Corrie ten Boom once said, "When the train goes through a tunnel and the world gets dark, do you jump out? Of course not. You sit still and trust the engineer to get you through."

When things are dark and you cannot see where you are at, or where you are going, trust the One who is engineering your life for the good (Romans 8:28). Trust Him when you are unable to track Him.

The Butterfly

In a beautiful city I visited there is a place called Butterfly

WILL I SURVIVE?

Gardens. It is set up to specifically show the vast array of butterflies in their developmental stages and habitat. It's gorgeous and breathtaking to see the hundreds of butterflies floating and fluttering around in the enclosed treed area. The butterfly in the following story accurately illustrates life struggles, which seem to come on a daily bases.

A man found a butterfly cocoon. One day, a small opening appeared. He sat and watched the butterfly for several hours as it struggled to force its body through the little hole.

Suddenly, the butterfly seemed to stop making progress. It appeared as if it had progressed as far as it could, and it could go no further. To help the butterfly the man took a small pair of scissors and snipped off the remaining bit of the protective cocoon. The butterfly then easily emerged; however, it had a swollen body and small, shriveled wings.

The man continued to watch the butterfly. He anticipated that at any moment, the wings would enlarge and expand to be able to support the body and fly away. Neither happened. In fact, the butterfly spent the rest of its short life, crawling around with a swollen body and shriveled wings. It would never fly.

The man, in his kindness and haste, did not realize that the restricting cocoon and the struggle required for the butterfly to get through the tiny opening was, in fact, God's way of forcing fluid from the body of the butterfly into its wings thus enabling it for flight once it achieved

WHATSOEVER HE SAYS

freedom from the cocoon.

Sometimes struggles are exactly what we need in our lives. If God allowed you to go through your life without any obstacles, it would spoil and cripple you. You would not be as strong as you could have been. You cannot fly without first developing wings!

Why, if God instantly changed us into what we are meant to be, we wouldn't even recognize ourselves! We wouldn't have the aptitude or the ability to help others along their way.

Perhaps you have read the following poem by an unknown author. It goes totally against our modern affluent society and the traditional church mentality of today. But there is great truth in these lines:

> I asked for Strength, and God gave me
> Difficulties to make me strong.
> I asked for Wisdom, and God gave me
> Problems to solve.
> I asked for Prosperity, and God gave me
> Brain and Brawn to work.
> I asked for Courage, and God gave me
> Danger to overcome.
> I asked for Love, and God gave me
> Troubled people to help.
> I asked for Favors, and God gave me Opportunities.
> I received nothing I wanted;
> I received everything I needed!

WILL I SURVIVE?

Whatever part of the process you find yourself in, keep loving God. Keep loving Him in and for all things. Remember, what happens to a man is less significant than what happens within him. The heart of the matter is our heart. It is far better to be poor and go to Heaven, than rich and go to Hell. Our eternal end is not found in this world. Therefore we ought to walk here and now full of love, peace and contentment in the knowledge of our Lord Jesus.

It is far better to be poor and go to Heaven, then rich and go to hell. The heart of the matter is our heart.

And we know that all things work together for good to those who love God, to those who are the called according to His purpose.
Romans 8:28

Mary

Here is a summation of the lesson and revelation from Mary, the mother of Jesus.

On the third day there was a wedding in Cana of Galilee, and the mother of Jesus was there. Now both Jesus and His disciples were invited to the wedding. And when they ran out of wine, the mother of Jesus said to Him, "They have no wine." Jesus said to her, "Woman, what does your concern have to do with Me? My hour has not yet come." His mother said to

WHATSOEVER HE SAYS

the servants, "Whatever He says to you, do it."
John 2:1-5

I have read this portion of scripture many times and only recently did God give me eyes to see what He was saying.

Modern times have softened and changed the stigma of pregnancy out of wedlock; however, it was not a pretty picture back in Jesus' day. Chances are, you could be killed by stoning, or, at a bare minimum, shunned, which was an awful experience to go through.

Of all people, Mary knew what happened to her. She was innocent. Her character, integrity and purity were all intact, but that was not what everyone else thought. People would believe in the stork before they would believe the line, *"God got me pregnant."* Really? You think that is going to go over well?

Suffice it to say, Mary lived with reproach for thirty very long years. Every day, at least for the first 29 years, people would talk, and boy can people talk! Still, Mary knew the truth, and one day she would be vindicated.

So day after day, rumor after rumor, facing judgment and condemning eyes, she lived her life. It was the same every day until the day of the marriage feast, when the party ran out of wine.

Now was the opportunity she had been waiting for. Jesus just had to do something spectacular. There was a large crowd from the village there, and what an opportue moment to be proven innocent in front of

WILL I SURVIVE?

them all.

So Mary walked up to Jesus and some hear her request, "They have no wine." There is communication going on between a mother and her Son that no one sees. Jesus knows what's being requested. He lived through the shame of the stories of being illegitimate. Many times he heard his mother cry herself to sleep over the hurtful things people can say.

The bottom line is: it's not about you.

Jesus also remembered the times he would sit with His Mother and she would talk about how special He was and that one day He would step forward as the Chosen One, the Messiah.

Yet here at the marriage feast in Cana of Galilee, Jesus turned to His mother and rebukes her? *"Woman, what does your concern have to do with Me? My hour has not yet come."* What just happened? Where is the love, compassion and understanding?

How often we pray and pray for the day Jesus will step onto the scene and answer our heart's cry. Remember, the process and the purpose of our lives is not about us. It is all about His will and way. We are not our own. We have been bought with a price (1 Corinthians 7:23) and have surrendered and submitted ourselves to His will and Word.

Do not get tripped up or bent out of shape by the way Jesus directs your life.

WHATSOEVER HE SAYS

"For My thoughts are not your thoughts, Nor are your ways My ways," says the LORD. "For as the heavens are higher than the earth, So are My ways higher than your ways, And My thoughts than your thoughts."
Isaiah 55:8-9

The Weakness of God

You will save yourself so much heartache, and have far less anxiety and frustration when you understand and make peace with the "weakness of God."

Because the foolishness of God is wiser than men, and the weakness of God is stronger than men.
1 Corinthians 1:25

Without going into great detail, the weakness of God occurs when you know what God can do, but yet He doesn't use His strength to do it. Jesus was crucified by the weakness of God. God could have sent 10,000 angels to stop His death, but He didn't. Yet, Jesus was resurrected by the power of God, the same power that could have prevented His death. When God shows up we see miracles, signs and wonders.

Keep in remembrance: God is on His throne, and all is well. He and He alone is sovereign and in control of all things. There is no other God besides Him alone (Isaiah 45:5, 8, 21-22). Our journey in life goes by His rules.

Listen to this revelatory statement Jesus made in

WILL I SURVIVE?

Matthew 11:6, *"And blessed is he who is not offended because of Me."* The word picture here is do not be tripped up, or bent out of shape because of the way Jesus directs your life. Bear in mind, that as a believer you are not your own; you have been bought with a price (1 Corinthians 6:20).

> **You are My friends if you do whatever I command you. John 15:14**

Jesus gave the rebuke. Mary was reminded of the purpose and her place in the process. She remembered in the beginning when the Angel of the Lord came to her and spoke the Word of God, and she responded with, *"Let it be to me according to Your Word"* (Luke 1:38).

Mary pondered and reflected on Jesus' response. "Okay. I really would like validation, but I have faith in God and will trust myself to His way, His Word and His timing, even if I have to wait another thirty years."

Then Mary turned to the servants and spoke her last words ever to be recorded in scripture, *"Whatever He says to you, do it"* (John 2:5). Wow! What a beautiful attitude and expression of understanding, confidence and trust. What a great testimony and example.

Talk about words to live by, as we go through the purpose and process called life. It's simple: **Whatever Jesus says to you, do it.** whatever Jesus says to you, do it. That can only be accomplished if your heart is knelt at the foot of the cross saying, *"never-the-less, not my will but thine be done."*

WHATSOEVER HE SAYS

Here is a profound proof text for all believers. It is the evidence of those who truly have a personal intimate relationship with the Lord Jesus: *if you keep His commandments*. The proof is in the pudding, and some puddings just don't taste too good. The recipe is off, and I'm not too sure which baker they are following.

Now by this we know that we know Him, if we keep His commandments. He who says, "I know Him," and does not keep His commandments, is a liar, and the truth is not in him.
1 John 2:3-4

Simon Peter was a fisherman. Fishermen know how to fish. He was good at what he did, or he would not be in the business. One day, Peter was out fishing. Amazing as it sounds, since he was a professional, he did not catch anything.

Then along comes Jesus, a carpenter, and tells the fisherman who has been fishing all night, to have another go at it. This time, just drop the net on the other side of the boat. Was He for real?

After the affront to his ability and livelihood, Peter makes this amazing comment: "Nevertheless, at Your Word I will let down the net." He simply takes Jesus at His Word, and obeys. Peter does what he's asked to do.

When He had stopped speaking, He said to Simon, "Launch out into the deep and let down your nets

WILL I SURVIVE?

for a catch." But Simon answered and said to Him, "Master, we have toiled all night and caught nothing; nevertheless at Your word I will let down the net." And when they had done this, they caught a great number of fish, and their net was breaking.
Luke 5:4-6

What a novel idea. Let God be God. What would happen if you let His Spirit and Word direct you each and every day?

Saul, whose name was changed to Paul, had a similar encounter with God back when he was persecuting the church.

So he [Saul], trembling and astonished, said, "Lord, what do You want me to do?" Then the Lord said to him, "Arise and go into the city, and you will be told what you must do."
Acts 9:6

Faith begets Faith. You cannot go into 9th grade until you pass 8th grade. In order for you to grow in faith, you must first learn to become obedient to what you do know you should do. As you are faithful in little, God can give you more (Matthew 25:14-30).

Therefore, to him who knows to do good and does not do it, to him it is sin.
James 4:17

WHATSOEVER HE SAYS

For precept must be upon precept, precept upon precept, Line upon line, line upon line, Here a little, there a little." For with stammering lips and another tongue He will speak to this people, To whom He said, "This is the rest with which You may cause the weary to rest," And, "This is the refreshing"; Yet they would not hear.
Isaiah 28:10-12

Six Water Pots

As we look back to the marriage in Cana of Galilee we see Jesus step into His destiny. He is in the perfect timing and will of God as He begins to give instruction to the servants.

Now there were set there six waterpots of stone, according to the manner of purification of the Jews, containing twenty or thirty gallons apiece. Jesus said to them, "Fill the waterpots with water." And they filled them up to the brim.
John 2:6-7

What were the instructions Jesus gave at the beginning of His earthly ministry and His very first miracle? *"Fill the waterpots"* to the brim. And the water was turned into wine.

We know from typology in 2 Corinthians 4:7 that earthen pots represent mankind. Humans are 98 percent water, and when God touches and fills you with His Spirit, there is truly a wonderful transformation that takes place. Water is turned to wine. The natural is now supernatural with God.

Jesus came to give you life, and that life more abundantly. I would suggest you have not really lived until you have willingly and gladly wrapped your hand in His and allowed Him to lead you where He may. You really don't have purpose until you have stepped into His purpose. There is no telling what can be accomplished for His Kingdom.

In Closing

Again, I ask you the questions I started with in this book. Have you ever gone through a time in your life when all seemed off balance and out of focus? A time when everything that could go wrong did? Frustration turned into alienation, which finally dipped into depression. What did you do when crisis hit, and made you feel imprisoned? Did you use the moment to seek God, or to mull over your misfortune and brood in silent anger? Your answer will determine your salvation or your demise.

God is at work. The real question is, will you let Him work? (Isaiah 43:13) Will you be submitted to the will and purpose of God? *"Be it unto me according to Your Word."* Will you be committed to His way and plan? *"Whatsoever He says, I will do."*

WHATSOEVER HE SAYS

What is so beautiful and encouraging and really motivates and invigorates me, is the fact that, for the church of the living God, the best is yet to come. The glory of the last day church will be greater than the first (Haggai 2:9). The best wine was given out at the end.

It really is your choice where you go to from here. Me, I do not want to come along after the miracle, signs and wonders are done. I want to be so close and involved with Jesus that when the miraculous happens, my hands are on it.

**As for me and my house, we will serve the LORD.
Joshua 24:15**

ABOUT THE AUTHOR

Bruce J. Bartel has preached the Gospel of Jesus for 39 years and functions as an international teacher, Christian counselor and therapist, mentor, pastor, missionary and evangelist. Bruce has traveled to 37 countries, and has lived in Canada, Europe and Asia. He attended Bible Colleges in Germany and England and two colleges in Canada.

purposeandprocess@gmail.com

Our Written Lives
book publishing services
www.owlofhope.com

CPSIA information can be obtained at www.ICGtesting.com
Printed in the USA
BVOW05s0627300315

393737BV00003B/5/P